Modern Critical Interpretations

Modern Critical Interpretations

Kurt Vonnegut's
Slaughterhouse-Five

Edited and with an introduction by
Harold Bloom
Sterling Professor of the Humanities
Yale University

CHELSEA HOUSE PUBLISHERS
Philadelphia

© 2001 by Chelsea House Publishers, a subsidiary of
Haights Cross Communications.

Introduction © 2001 by Harold Bloom.

Printed and bound in the United States of America

10 9 8 7 6 5 4 3 2 1

∞ The paper used in this publication meets the minimum
requirements of the American National Standard for
Permanence of Paper for Printed Library Materials,
Z39.48-1984

Library of Congress Cataloging-in-Publication Data

Kurt Vonnegut's Slaughterhouse-Five / Harold Bloom, editor.
    p. cm. — (Modern Critical Interpretations)
  Includes bibliographical references and index.
  ISBN 0-7910-5925-1 (alk. paper)
  1. Vonnegut, Kurt. Slaugherhouse-Five. 2. Science
fiction, American—History and criticism. I. Title:
Slaugherhouse-Five. II. Bloom, Harold. III. Series.
  PS3572.O5 S6355 2000
  813'.54—dc21   00-059628

Chelsea House Publishers
1974 Sproul Road, Suite 400
Broomall, PA 19008-0914

The Chelsea House World Wide Web address is
http://www.chelseahouse.com

Contributing Editor: Aaron Tillman

Produced by: Robert Gerson Publisher's Services, Santa Barbara, CA

Contents

Editor's Note

My Introduction is a brief appreciation of *Slaughterhouse-Five*, emphasizing its autobiographical matrix.

Peter J. Reed begins the chronological sequence of critiques by arguing that Vonnegut's novel "actually possesses an intricately designed structure," after which Peter G. Jones centers upon the character and function of Billy Pilgrim as Vonnegut's warrior against technology.

For James Lundquist, Vonnegut himself is the most fully developed character in *Slaughterhouse-Five*, while the requirements of chaos are emphasized by Robert Merrill and Peter A. Scholl.

Lawrence R. Broer exploring schizophrenia in the book sees *Slaughterhouse-Five* as the culmination of a Pilgrim's Progress, after which Leonard Mustazza intimates that the novel longs for a return of Eden.

Vonnegut qualifies as a witness, presumably in Eli Wiesel's sense, in the judgment of William Rodney Allen, while Jerome Klinkowitz shrewdly emphasizes the "public spokesmanship" of Vonnegut's personal style.

Introduction

On December 19, 1944, Kurt Vonnegut was captured by the Germans during the Battle of the Bulge; he was 22 years old. Sent to Dresden, he survived the firebombing of the city on February 13–14, 1945, in which 135,000 Germans were killed. That is the biographical context (in part) for the novel, *Slaughterhouse-Five, or The Children's Crusade* (1969).

Since Vonnegut had begun publishing novels in 1952, it is clear that nearly a quarter-century had to go by before the trauma of 1945 could be transmuted into the exorcism of *Slaughterhouse-Five*. I have just reread the novel after thirty years, remembering my shocked admiration for it when it first appeared, and not looking forward to encountering it again. As it should, *Slaughterhouse-Five* remains a very disturbed and disturbing book, and still moves me to troubled admiration. I prefer *Cat's Cradle*, but *Slaughterhouse-Five* may prove to be an equally permanent achievement.

The shadow of Céline's *Journey to the End of the Night* never quite leaves Vonnegut's starker works, including *Slaughterhouse-Five*. I myself read the anti-Semitic Céline with loathing; one sees what is strong in the writing, but a Jewish literary critic is hardly Céline's ideal audience. So it goes.

It is difficult to comment upon *Slaughterhouse-Five* without being contaminated by its styles and procedures, which is necessarily a tribute to the book. In "structure" (an absurd term to apply to almost any novel by Vonnegut), *Slaughterhouse-Five* is a whirling medley, and yet it all coheres. Billy Pilgrim, as a character, does not cohere, but that is appropriate, since his schizophrenia (to call it that) is central to the book.

The planet Tralfamadore, where Billy enjoys pneumatic bliss with Montana Wildhack, is certainly preferable to a world of Nazi death camps and Dresden firebombings. The small miracle of *Slaughterhouse-Five* is that it could be composed at all. Vonnegut always writes from the survivor's stance, where all laughter has to be a step away from madness or fury. So indeed it goes.

1

Somewhere in the book, the Tralfamadorians tell Billy Pilgrim that their flying-saucer crews had verified the presence of seven sexes on Earth, all of them necessary if babies are to go on being born. I think that is one of the useful moral observations I will keep in mind whenever I recall *Slaughterhouse-Five*.

PETER J. REED

The End of the Road:
Slaughterhouse-Five, or The Children's Crusade

In *Slaughterhouse-Five* (1969), Vonnegut comes at last to a direct confrontation with his Dresden experience. He also brings together many of the other things he has talked about in his first five novels. The numerous recapitulations of previous themes, resurrections of characters who have appeared before, and recollections of earlier mentioned incidents in this novel are not just self-parody as they might be in *Cat's Cradle*, nor are they simply the development of a kind of extended in-joke as they might be in the intervening novels. Rather, they represent an attempt at integration, an effort to bring together all that Vonnegut has been saying about the human condition and contemporary American society, and to relate those broad commentaries to the central traumatic, revelatory and symbolic moment of the destruction of Dresden. The event itself, of course, is not the problem. The difficulty lies in trying to say all that the fire-raid means, to one man, to each individual man, to all men collectively. Vonnegut also says the book is a failure. We may not agree; or, if we do, we will probably want to give more credit to the attempt than the author gives himself. The only real failure is that the novel had to be written at all. Whatever its weaknesses (like characterization, a weakness Vonnegut freely admits), the book's achievements are considerable—and more numerous than a first glance suggests. *Slaughterhouse-Five* goes beyond being a theraputically autobiographical novel,

From *Kurt Vonnegut, Jr.* © 1972 by Warner Books, Inc.

or simply an anti-war novel, the two categories into which it could be most easily fitted. It is both these things and more—an attempt, in effect, to create a contemporary legend.

Slaughterhouse-Five begins autobiographically with Vonnegut musing about himself—his good friend the dog, late nights drinking, smoking, telephoning long lost friends, teaching at the Writers' Workshop at the University of Iowa—and the fact that he has been telling people for a long time that he was working on a book about the raid on Dresden. He was there during that raid, and its impression has been indelible. He also recalls visiting a veteran friend, "Bernard V. O'Hare," to talk over some of their war experiences. O'Hare's wife, Mary, had appeared hostile, and it emerged that she had feared the book would be a glorification of war, adaptable to a movie starring John Wayne or Frank Sinatra. She had insisted the men were "babies" in the war, and that a glorification would send more children, like theirs upstairs, into more wars. That was when the author agreed to call his story *The Children's Crusade*. With O'Hare he then traveled to Dresden on Guggenheim Fellowship money, looking back like Lot's wife at the ruined city. The book is a failure, he says, because it is written by a pillar of salt.

After this prologue, Vonnegut recounts the story of Billy Pilgrim, focusing upon his capture by the Germans in World War II, his presence in Dresden during the raid, and the consequences of these experiences on his later life. It should be emphasized that the novel does not at all follow the chronological development used in this summary for clarification. Basically there are two major time-streams in the novel; from Billy's becoming lost in Luxembourg in 1944 to his being in Dresden in 1945, and from 1968 to later in the same year. But there are numerous time shifts between these two sequences and to other periods. Seldom do more than two pages fix on one date.

Billy Pilgrim, like his author, was born in 1922. One of his earliest memories is of being taught to swim by his father on the "sink if you don't" system. Other early traumatic experiences occur during a trip West with his family. While he stands tremulously on the brink of the Grand Canyon his mother unexpectedly touches him and he wets his pants. Then he has the life scared out of him when the guide turns out the lights in the Carlsbad Caverns.

After a few unsuccessful weeks in college, Billy goes off to war as a chaplain's assistant. In 1944 the Germans pour into Luxembourg during the Battle of the Bulge, leaving Billy stranded behind enemy lines. He meets up with two scouts and a tank gunner named Roland Weary. For several days this motley foursome searches hopefully for American lines, Billy bobbing up and down on a heel-less shoe. Under the stress of hunger, shock, exhaustion and exposure, Billy loses the will to live and his mind wanders. It is here that he begins to become "unstuck in time"—that is, to find himself living in moments of the past or future. From this point on he frequently knows what will or will not happen to him.

Eventually Billy's slow pace and apparent delirium become too much for the scouts, who depart on their own. This infuriates Weary, who sets about beating up Billy, only being prevented from finishing the job by the arrival of some German irregular soldiers. Weary is forced to give up his shoes in exchange for the feet-cutting hinged clogs of one of the Germans. The two hobbling Americans are herded off to join an ever increasing number of other prisoners being marched into Germany. They are jammed into boxcars, which, after sitting in marshalling yards for two days, begin a slow journey toward the east. On the ninth day, Weary dies of gangrene from his injured feet. He blames Pilgrim for his plight, and a paranoid little soldier named Paul Lazzaro swears to avenge him by having Billy killed.

Eventually the dilapidated prisoners are unloaded at a camp for Russian POWs, are deloused, showered, given overcoats, and marched into a compound for British officers at the center of the camp. The British POWs are organized, clean, healthy and disciplined, and put on a welcome dinner and pantomime for the new arrivals. The food overwhelms the half-starved Americans, whose unsanitary physical response and general dispiritedness appall the Englishmen. Billy spends a couple of days in the British sickquarters, time-travelling as usual.

Within a few days the Americans march into Dresden to begin work, mainly bottling a honey-like vitamin supplement for pregnant women. They are housed in a slaughterhouse numbered five. At one point they are urged to join the "Free America Corps" to fight the Russians by the American Quisling, Howard Campbell. When the great air raid begins, Campbell, four guards and a hundred of the Americans take shelter in a deep cold storage area. They survive while 135,000 are dying above. When they surface, the ruins of Dresden look like the face of the moon. For a few days the Americans are employed digging in the wreckage. One of them, the earnest former school-teacher Edgar Derby, is executed by a firing squad for taking a teapot from a wrecked building. As the war ends, Billy and his friends are riding around Dresden in a coffin-shaped horse drawn wagon. Billy basks in the sunlight, contentedly time-travelling.

After repatriation, Billy goes to optometrists' school in Ilium. There he meets and marries the college founder's daughter, Valencia. She is a gross, candy-munching woman of limited intellect, but she loves Billy and the two lead a fairly contented life together. They have two children, Barbara and Robert. Robert goes through a period of juvenile delinquency, but emerges as an exemplary Green Beret. Barbara becomes a "bitchy flibbertigibbet" fussing over her father and her husband. Billy thrives as an optometrist, coming eventually to employ five assistants, own shares in other local businesses, earn $60,000 a year, and drive a Cadillac complete with Birch Society bumper stickers supplied by his father-in-law. He continues to time travel, often at moments disconcerting to his patients, so in 1948 he commits himself to a mental hospital. There he shares a ward with Eliot Rosewater, who introduces him to Kilgore Trout's science fiction. Years later, Billy actually meets Kilgore Trout. He discovers the writer ruthlessly supervising a crew of newspaper boys, and invites Trout to his wedding anniversary party.

By 1967, Billy seldom seems to know whether he is here or there—or now or then. On the night of his daughter's wedding he is picked up, as he knows he will be, by a Tralfamadorian flying saucer. Transported to Tralfamadore, he is kept in a luxurious "zoo" where he is mated with a kidnapped movie star, Montana Wildhack. (Billy's absence escapes notice, because by travelling through a time warp his stay of several years on Tralfamadore only means that he is gone from Earth for a microsecond.) The two live almost blissfully, have a child, and then somehow Billy returns. The Tralfamadorians explain Billy's time travelling. To them all times coexist— "whatever is always has been and always will be"—meaning, among other things, that people are always alive at some point in time. They necessarily believe in inevitability and see the conception of free will as a curious Earthling perversion.

In 1968, Billy survives an airplane crash, but with a serious head wound which again hospitalizes him. As the distraught Valencia races to the hospital, she becomes involved in a car accident which rips the exhaust pipes from the Cadillac. On arrival she collapses of carbon monoxide poisoning and dies almost immediately. This time Billy shares his ward with Air Force historian Bertram Copeland Rumfoord, who is writing on the Dresden raid. After his release, Billy visits New York where he goes on a radio talk show to divulge his experiences with the Tralfamadorians. This, and the letters on the same subject he writes to newspapers, convinces his daughter Barbara that he is, at 46, senile.

As Billy sees what happens subsequently, he becomes something of a celebrity, speaking to large crowds about flying saucers, time, and the insignificance of death. On February 13, 1976 (the twenty-first anniversary of the Dresden raid), he is speaking in a stadium in Chicago. (Chicago has been rebuilt, having been hydrogen-bombed by the Chinese. The U.S.A. has been Balkanized into twenty petty nations to end its threat to world peace.) He predicts that he will die within the hour, makes no effort to prevent this, and is shot by a gunman hired by the aged, crazy, but still revengeful Paul Lazzaro.

Vonnegut returns to his exterior frame for the story at the end, mentioning the deaths of Senator Robert F. Kennedy, Martin Luther King, his father, and the weekly carnage in Vietnam. He muses that Darwin teaches that "those who die are meant to die, that corpses are improvements." As he and O'Hare fly toward Dresden, he reflects that if the Tralfamadorians are right that we all live forever it does not delight him, but that he is glad to have many happy moments to relive. O'Hare observes that by the year 2,000 the world population will be seven billion. And the author, having given such a bleak portrayal of the individual human's lot on Earth, says sardonically, "I suppose they will all want dignity."

Since the Dresden raid is central to this novel and often mentioned by Vonnegut, here is an historical note. Contrary to some claims, Dresden was *not* an open city, and it did present some targets of military significance. But it had not been bombed before, and the great raid killed few military personnel. At the time, Dresden's population had been doubled by refugees from the East. On the night of February 13–14, about 800 Royal Air Force Lancaster heavy bombers struck in two waves, dropping tons of high explosive bombs and 650,000 incendiaries. The enormous conflagration created was visible 200 miles away. The next day, 450 American B-17 Fortresses dropped more bombs, and P-51 Mustang fighters strafed the wrecked city. Militarily, the raid was immensely successful, very few allied aircraft being shot down while the target was virtually destroyed. Casualties were variously estimated from 35,000 to over 200,000. 135,000, the conservative estimate of the Dresden Police President, is the normally accepted figure. Whether Dresden should have been bombed at all, especially so late in the war, has been questioned. The allies kept details of the raid secret long after.

While *Slaughterhouse-Five* may appear to be wandering and random, an example of Vonnegut's tendencies toward the episodic and the digressive indulged to the extreme, it actually possesses an intricately designed structure. The author's description of his efforts to outline this story, climaxed by his making his "prettiest one" on the back of a roll of wallpaper with his daughter's crayons, seems entirely appropriate. Billy Pilgrim is at one point described as trying to reinvent or restructure his life, while in telling the story Vonnegut tries to give form to the same experiences. At the center of Vonnegut's material—in the wallpaper outline it is cross-hatched across the sheet—is the Dresden raid. From that central event he extends a web outward in time, space and characters. But "web" is a poor metaphor; one might as easily say that he "tunnels into" the experience to find its meaning. Time, space and event coexist and coalesce in this novel, and that is what the structure attempts to convey.

First Vonnegut sets up a frame for the story with the autobiographical prologue in the first chapter. An important preparation for this comes on the title page itself; between the title and a thumbnail biography of the author, Vonnegut describes his book as "A Duty Dance with Death." The autobiographical first chapter is matched by a return to more of the same in the last chapter, completing the frame, but in such a way as to integrate the frame with the main narrative. The framing device and the interrelationship of the autobiographical with the narrative are strengthened by periodic intrusions by the author throughout the novel: "I was there" or "that was me." "A Dance" is an apt description for the interwoven pattern of the narrative, with the author himself occasionally appearing as one of the dancers. All of the events portrayed are carefully interconnected, and events from "separate" times are often juxtaposed, completing or commenting upon one another. The frequent complementary nature of the time fragments adds to their coherence, although there is surprisingly little difficulty in following this seemingly disjointed narrative. The prologue to the first chapter, and the quick general guidelines to Billy's life in the second, provide the reader with a strong sense of direction from the outset.

The title page gives another clue to the structure of *Slaughterhouse-Five*: "This is a novel somewhat in the telegraphic schizophrenic manner of tales of the planet Tralfamadore, where the flying saucers come from." It might seem absurd to take such an obviously spoofing account at all seriously. The description of the Tralfamadorian novel represents characteristic Vonnegutian self-derision, like the portraits of Kilgore Trout, but as parody it makes some real sense. The Tralfamadorian novel is made up of "clumps of symbols" each of which "'is a brief, urgent message— describing a situation, a scene.'" Tralfamadorians read these simultaneously, not consecutively. "'There isn't any particular relationship between all the messages, except that the author has chosen them carefully, so that, when seen all at once, they produce an image of life that is beautiful and inspiring and deep.'" Aside from the fact that the Tralfamadorians, in their novels as in their minds, emphasize beautiful moments and exclude the unpleasant ones, *Slaughterhouse-Five* almost fits their requirements. Most of the situations described are grim, many downright painful. The "clumps of symbols" obviously cannot be read simultaneously, either, but the way in which short scenes from several points in time are spliced together does help sustain the impression of concurrent actions, and intensifies the sense of an interrelationship of events transcending time. Nor is there always a "particular relationship between all the messages," but they often do show a kinship of theme or image, and they cohere to create "an image of life" which, while not always "beautiful," is frequently "surprising" and in total effect quite "deep." Because all of its scenes cannot be read simultaneously, the book comes closer to possessing a climax than does the Tralfamadorian novel. It is hard to single out one climactic event, be it the raid itself or the ironic execution of Edgar Derby, but the novel certainly builds toward the end where the meaning, the questions and the emotional impact come together.

In order that this discussion itself avoid the "telegraphic schizophrenic manner," it might be well to pay attention first to the nucleus of the novel, namely Billy Pilgrim and his experiences during the war, in the Dresden raid, and on his trip to Tralfamadore. As already mentioned, there are limitations to the characterization of Billy; limitations which seem to go beyond those explained by Vonnegut at one point in the novel. "There are almost no characters in this story," he says, "and almost no dramatic confrontations, because most of the people in it are so sick and so much the listless playthings of enormous forces. One of the main effects of war, after all, is that people are discouraged from being characters." Some of that we can accept, but some we may question. Vonnegut makes the point here that Edgar Derby is about to act as a character. Others, like the British officers, Weary, and even Paul Lazzaro, become "characters" as opposed to "listless playthings" apparently *because* of this confrontation with war situations. The circumstances imposed do seem to lessen the possibilities of "dramatic confrontations," most of the characters *are* sick, and many of them are manipulated by "enormous forces" in ways which limit their freedom for character defining actions. Furthermore, the whole design of the novel calls for much of the cast to make only brief appearances which, while they might create striking impressions, are not of the sort to develop characterizations. Yet most of these observations do not really apply to the protagonist.

Billy Pilgrim is both sick and a listless plaything, but that part of his characterization works quite well. His physical ailments and his vulnerability to controlling forces are even more extensive than those of Eliot Rosewater in *God Bless You, Mr. Rosewater*, and impose some of the same burdens on characterization, yet in this respect Billy seems at least as convincing as Eliot. The ambiguities of his sanity or insanity are more extreme than those surrounding Eliot. They represent the culmination of a progression which begins with Paul Proteus' moral uncertainty, which becomes psychologically more complex in the uncertain truths of Howard Campbell's self-analyses, and which incorporates questions of morality, motivations and sanity in the case of Eliot Rosewater. The very uncertainties and ambiguities of Billy Pilgrim as shocked, uncomprehending and listless victim add conviction to his characterization in that role. Billy grinning foolishly at Germans who abuse him, Billy in a delirium of fatigue in the boxcar, even Billy weeping silently years after the war, emerges as touchingly lifelike. In other roles he does not.

Perhaps the problem arises from the number of roles Billy must fulfill. The novel concerns itself not just with Dresden or the war, but with a much broader depiction of a human condition which these events emblematize. At the center of such a work, Billy becomes, as his name distinctly suggests, a contemporary pilgrim progressing through an absurd world—except that he does not really progress. Being an Everyman proves tricky in the age of specialization. Billy must be innocent Adam falling into the terrible wisdom of the twentieth century. He portrays a modern version of the Christ figure more than once. He is the child duped into the children's crusade. He becomes a credulous and adaptable Gulliver on a voyage to another world. And he is asked to fulfill the roles of prosperous businessman, polished convention speaker, crank participant in talk shows, and death-denigrating messiah of quasi-religious crusades. Understandably, his characterization proves unequal to all these roles. Eliot Rosewater's recovery from shell shock to become successful foundation administrator seems plausible enough; it simply marks a return to his established life style. His becoming benefactor to the poor similarly has adequate motivation. It proves much more difficult to reconcile the predominant image of Billy the bemused POW with the $60,000-a-year optometrist-businessman, even given that he married the boss's daughter. Vonnegut asks us to give him that—and to laboriously document Billy's ascending career would indeed be irrelevant to the novel's purposes. We might ask *why* Billy must become a $60,000-a-year optometrist, unless it is to emphasize the helpless child at the mercy of indomitable forces within the controlling businessman. Or unless, of course, the $60,000-a-year optometrist *is* the modern Everyman. We do know that Billy weeping silently, dozing off into time travel, blundering embarrassedly in a porno bookstore, or jiggling on his electronic bed fits consistently with the shattered soldier, and that it is hard to see how a chap like that could successfully run even a shoeshine stand. Shell-shocked veterans have made competent businessmen. Henry Green shows how in *Back*, and Vonnegut makes it plausible with Eliot Rosewater, but the chamber of commerce side of Billy Pilgrim never comes alive.

At the core of the characterization of Billy Pilgrim is the conception of war as a children's crusade. The starting point for this analogy is Mary O'Hare's insistence that men like to give war an aura of glamor as a mature masculine activity whereas in fact it is fought by mere babies. The author concurs—"We *had* been foolish virgins in the war, right at the end of childhood." And his promise to call the book "The Children's Crusade" leads him and Bernard O'Hare to look up some facts about the title event. They discover that the Children's Crusade began in 1213, the idea of two monks who planned to assemble an army of children and sell them as slaves in North

Africa. Accordingly, 30,000 volunteer children were marched to Marseilles, half subsequently being drowned in shipwrecks and half indeed being sold into slavery. A few went to Genoa, where there were no ships waiting, and were treated kindly by the local people. The obvious parallels with the raising of a modern army are that the people sent to die are in both cases young, innocent, and uncomprehending, that the patriotic fervor of onlookers and influential persons urges on both enterprises, that too many die needlessly while too few are treated humanely, and that the declared "noble" intentions may bear little relation to the actual purposes or accomplishments of the enterprise. In each case, mere children find themselves the hapless pawns of forces they neither understand nor can resist. Young of face, gawky of stature and childishly perplexed, Billy Pilgrim, who like the crusader starts out on a holy mission as chaplain's assistant, makes the perfect representational figure for this conception of war.

The affinity between men at war and children emerges in several ways. Among the most obvious is the youth of Billy himself and of other soldiers. Two German troopers, in particular, are merely boys in their teens. The colonel who commands the British prisoners makes the point explicit, saying that having been prisoners since the beginning of hostilities, his group had imagined the war being fought by men of their age. After he sees the Americans shaved and cleaned, he realizes for the first time how young they are and is shocked. "'My God, my God—' I said to myself, 'it's the Children's Crusade.'" Vonnegut underlines the resemblance more than once, as when he qualifies his description of "Wild Bob's" regiment as about forty-five hundred men by saying "—a lot of children, actually." The character of "Wild Bob" helps make another observation on children at war: that men at war become as children in fact if they are not in age. This colonel from Wyoming has always wanted his men to call him "Wild Bob" (they never have), as if he boyishly envisions himself fulfilling the role of a military "character," hero and friend to his troops—whom he has in fact led to disaster. Similarly, Roland Weary wistfully envisions himself as one of "the Three Musketeers," and dreams romantically of valor and loyalty. The two scouts will not play his game. Fittingly, the entertainment the Englishmen provide for the Americans is a modified children's pantomime, and when the British recoil from their "guests" they divide the camp compound by the old childhood technique of scraping a groove in the ground with the heel. These and similar instances emphasize the childlike nature of men at war not so much to say that war is childish as to indicate the haplessness of men caught up in war, like children somehow swept up in an adult barroom brawl. They also suggest that men made helpless, shocked, dazed, bullied and maimed in war are driven back

into themselves in regressive ways. War *might* be childish in some ways—
the referees of the American war games arguing over who is "dead," or the
Germans "capturing" for the cameras the already captive Billy could be
taken to suggest this—but that is not the main thrust of Vonnegut's anti-war
theme. He seems most concerned to show war as a terrifying unleashing of
monstrous forces which sweeps up the innocent children of men to destroy
and enslave them.

That particular emphasis to Vonnegut's war-criticism, and beyond that
to his diagnosis of the contemporary human condition, necessitates that he
extend—even mythicize—his presentation of Billy Pilgrim as universal man-
child. The name begins the job, and the allusions to Jesus Christ and Adam
continue it. One of Trout's novels, *The Gospel from Outer Space*, sets the tone
and the direction of the Christ references. Trout's spaceman, having studied
Christianity, finds it hard to understand how Christians can so easily be cruel.
He concludes that whereas the Gospels *mean* to teach mercy to even the
lowest of things, they actually taught this: *"Before you kill somebody, make
absolutely sure he isn't well connected."* Consequently, the modern reader of the
Gospels comes to the story of men killing the Son of God and thinks that the
killers made a mistake, as if killing Jesus had he *not* been the Son of God
would have been all right. The spaceman's gospel has God take a different
line: *"From this moment on, He will punish horribly anybody who torments a bum
who has no connections!"* Soldier Billy, if not Businessman Billy, fills the role of
bum-Jesus admirably, and makes an excellent vehicle for the demonstration
of those morals about showing mercy to even the lowest.

Other Christ allusions show Billy wandering in a wilderness, being
falsely accused and made a scapegoat (by Weary, who blames Pilgrim for his
death), being reviled by the other inmates of the boxcar, and hanging from a
crossbar in one corner, "self-crucified." Later, as he lies dozing in the cart after
the Dresden raid, he hears voices which sound to him like "the tones . . . used
by the friends of Jesus when they took His ruined body down from His cross."
Ironically, those tones are not meant for him but for the pathetic horses
drawing the cart. Billy cries for those horses, and weeps often later, always
silently. Vonnegut observes that "in *that* respect, at least, he resembled the
Christ of the carol: *The cattle are lowing / The Baby awakes. / But the little Lord
Jesus / No crying He makes."* (That carol also provides the novel's epigraph.)
Vonnegut's saying "in *that* respect, at least," implies his rather self-consciously
putting a qualification on the Christ role of Billy, but that he definitely does
intend Billy to be viewed thus in *at least that* one respect. The identification can
be taken seriously if not solemnly. At times it becomes ludicrous—but that is
exactly the point. Billy's being moonishly bemused, utterly helpless, even
ridiculous, fits him for the role of persecuted child, of babe born to die.

Perhaps the most important allusion to Adam comes at the time of Billy's capture. The German corporal wears a pair of golden cavalry boots taken from a Hungarian colonel. As he waxes them, he tells recruits, "'If you look in there deep enough, you'll see Adam and Eve.'" Obviously the only way that could happen would be for a recruit to see the Adam and Eve within himself, which is essentially what Billy does when he sees the naked couple within the boots' lustre. "They were so innocent, so vulnerable, so eager to behave decently. Billy Pilgrim loved them." Innocent, vulnerable, eager to please—the description applies aptly to Billy. When the fifteen year old German soldier is labelled "as beautiful as Eve," the association of Billy with Adam becomes even stronger. This allusion, like those to Christ, has its comic undercutting. The nearest Billy comes to being Adam in a literal sense might be when he and Montana Wildhack live naked in the geodesic paradise of the Tralfamadorian zoo. But while these identifications are made almost laughingly, as the tone of the novel demands, they are explicit. They extend the dimensions and significance of Billy's role, contributing to the expansion of the book to a more universal scope than that of anti-war novel alone.

The character of Billy gives *Slaughterhouse-Five* a point of focus, particularly for the emotions generated by the wide ranging action of the story. In that respect, this novel proves more successful than *Cat's Cradle* which in several ways resembles *Slaughterhouse-Five* more closely than do the other four novels. (*Cat's Cradle* also speaks of the Children's Crusade, of mass destruction, war and the moral questions they generate, uses numerous references to other works by Vonnegut, and spreads itself over a similar wide range of times, episodes, and social issues.) The war, and Dresden in particular, also gives focus, in a way which again invites contrast to *Cat's Cradle*. The narrative device used in that novel is that Jonah has been trying to write about "the day the world ended"—the day Hiroshima was bombed— but has been unable to do so. He does ultimately write about the day the world ends, but the final catastrophe by *ice-nine*, while giving tone to the narrative and providing the context for the considerations of ethics, religion, politics and art, does not become a dominating event in itself. The Dresden raid does achieve such centrality in *Slaughterhouse-Five*. Everything that happens points forward or backward to Dresden. If the war becomes the general metaphor for Vonnegut's vision of the human condition, Dresden becomes the symbol, the quintessence. It acts as something concrete, a specific point of reference, to which all that is said about human behavior or the nature of man's existence can be related. For example, who better fitted to ask that recurring question "Why me?" than the victims—or the survivors—of Dresden? Or what better example of the absurd than this, the Allies' most "successful" application of bombing in the European theater, being directed at a non-target? The Dresden raid, together with the character of Billy Pilgrim, helps unify and focus the disparate elements of the novel. As an actual event realistically portrayed, the raid adds intensity to the questions, denunciations, and pathos in the novel, as compared to that generated by fictional disasters in the earlier books. That fact also greatly affects the tone of the novel, making it more serious, more terrifying and more moving than *Cat's Cradle*.

The moral and psychological context for the depiction of the Dresden raid is set up in the first chapter. There we see essentially two perspectives; the highly personal recollections of the author who was involved in the event, and the detached, distant view of history. The latter is introduced in the account of the destruction of Sodom and Gomorrah which the author reads in his motel Gideon Bible. It suggests that "Those were vile people in both those cities, as is well known. The world was better off without them." Obviously, he does not share that harsh moral view, and his sympathies lie with Lot's wife who looks back to where people and homes had been—an act he finds lovable because it is so human. The Biblical account provides a precedent for Dresden; a city destroyed in righteous wrath, people judged evil and ripe for annihilation, and an observer who looks back wonderingly, touched by human compassion. Some of the parallel moral questions posed by such great destructions are obvious. So the people of Sodom and Gomorrah were a bad lot—does that justify their obliteration? So the Germans had devastated Warsaw, Rotterdam, Coventry and East London, and had sent millions to their deaths in other ways—does that make moral the destruction of Dresden? Vonnegut makes considerable effort to incorporate official and historical assessments of such raids into his novel by quoting from President Truman's announcement of the atom-bombing of Hiroshima and from David Irving's book, *The Destruction of Dresden*. The Truman statement, made in time of war, essentially argues that the destruction of Hiroshima was necessary to save civilization from the destruction wreaked by the Japanese. The two forwards to Irving's book, written by Lieutenant General Ira C. Eaker, U.S.A.F., and Air Marshal Sir Robert Saundby, R.A.F., some time after the war, struggle with the moral issues, regretting so many deaths in a militarily unnecessary raid but insisting that they be viewed in the context of the even more massive slaughters wrought by the Germans.

Vonnegut's comment on these official assessments comes in the rambling words of Billy Pilgrim: "If you're ever in Cody, Wyoming . . . just ask for Wild Bob." Wild Bob was the colonel who had led his troops to disaster, lost his regiment, then tried to assure his soldiers they had "nothing to be ashamed of" because they had left a lot of Germans dead, too. Yet Wild Bob remains a sympathetic character. Perhaps through him Vonnegut observes that military men responsible for such slaughters act not out of malignity but from muddled values which prevent them from seeing simpler moral truths. Treated less sympathetically than the commander who makes a mistake is the military historian who later tries to justify the error. Illustrating this role is Bertram Copeland Rumfoord, "the official Air Force historian," writing his one volume history of the U.S.A.A.F. in World War II. He feels obliged to mention Dresden because so many people now know that it was worse than Hiroshima. The raid has been cloaked in secrecy for years lest it be criticized by "a lot of bleeding hearts," Rumfoord says, and he seems bent only on dismissing any notion that it might be a blemish on the glorious record of the Air Force. So intent is he on treating Dresden with official "detachment" that he shuts out any possible firsthand reports from Billy Pilgrim. He seems only concerned to convince Billy, as his readers, that "it *had* to be done"—while remaining rather uneasy himself.

Posed against the official assessments are episodes involving two lesser characters which serve to expose Dresden to a different moral viewpoint. The Sodom and Gomorrah reference, the allusion to Hiroshima and the historical judgments on Dresden all involve looking at the raid from a distance, taking an overview of it, placing it in a large historical context. The stories of Paul Lazarro and Edgar Derby, like those of Lot's wife and Billy Pilgrim, reverse the perspective, measuring the larger event against individual human consequences. Paul Lazarro typifies those miserable little men, inviting our pity as much as our disgust, who are as close as Vonnegut ever gets to creating villains. He threatens to have Billy killed, and actually does have him killed years later. In the prison camp he tries to steal an English officer's watch, gets caught in the act, and suffers a severe mauling. Characteristically, he swears he will have the Englishman killed—a stranger will knock at his door, announce he comes from Paul Lazarro, "shoot his pecker off," give him a couple of minutes to think about that, then kill him. He also tells a tender story of how he once fed a dog steak containing sharpened fragments of clocksprings. This twisted little crank feeds on revenge—"the sweetest thing in life"—yet he takes no satisfaction from the destruction of Dresden. He bears the Germans no grudge, and he prides himself on never harming an innocent bystander. The obvious moral object lesson here is that in some ways even a sordid monster like Lazarro can be superior to the saviors of civilization, who also take revenge, who kill those who have done them no harm in ways every bit as horrible as anything the warped mind of Lazarro could conceive and with no thought for innocent bystanders. The second incident involves Edgar Derby, who is arrested and shot by the Germans for plundering when caught with a perfectly ordinary teapot taken from a ruined house. This time we observe the irony of a society which condones massive destruction but which executes a man—one who tries bravely to be decent and moral—for salvaging a teapot from that wreckage.

These two minor incidents give scale to the inhumanity and moral dubiousness of the Dresden raid. The disaster itself remains so massive as to be hard to register in any other way. Statistics of the numbers killed and the houses destroyed, or descriptions of the ruins lying like the surface of the moon, remain too large, too general, too abstract. Particular images like human bodies reduced to charred logs or girls boiled alive in a water tower, and personal episodes like those involving Lazarro and Derby, stick in the mind. The same is true for Billy. The horror of the total nightmare registers in the little things, like the four distraught German guards, huddled together, mouths open but not knowing what to say, looking like a barbershop quartet singing (and here the irony borders on excess) "That Old Gang of Mine." "'So long forever,' old sweethearts and pals—God bless 'em—.'" And after all that he has suffered and the carnage he has witnessed among the debris, it takes the sight of those wretched horses drawing his cart to reduce Billy to tears.

The significance of the Dresden firestorm, then, is weighed on the scale of time, from Sodom and Gomorrah down to Hiroshima, and on the scale of human response, from the collective, public view of the official history to the personal nightmare of Billy Pilgrim. It is also measured spatially, in effect, through the perspective afforded by the use of science fiction. Billy tells the Tralfamadorians about wars on Earth, and what a great threat to all life the inhabitants of his planet must be. The Tralfamadorians regard his concerns as stupid. They know how the Universe ends, and Earth has nothing to do with it. Their own experiments with flying-saucer fuels end the Universe. In any case, they tell Billy, Tralfamadore is not as peaceful as he seems to think. They have wars as dreadful as anything Billy knows about. Once again the point of view of a more sophisticated being from another planet provides commentary on human behavior, yet this time it might surprise us as much as it does Billy. The Tralfamadorians' timeless view is not that Earthlings are senseless and barbaric to engage in war, a menace to themselves and the Universe. It is that Billy is ridiculous to expect such a logical projection of the future to work in an absurd Universe, and that he exaggerates the importance of the human role in the cosmos. In particular, he overemphasizes free will and fails to recognize that the tragedies of war and ultimate destruction occur, like all things, because that is the way the moment is structured. They advocate acceptance of life's cruelties and catastrophes, saying "so it goes" to each, then turning their thoughts to happier things.

That position has a certain undeniable logic, especially to beings capable of time-travel. For one thing, it avoids putting them constantly at odds with the essential nature of an Absurd Universe. For another, it makes sense given their conception of time, where past, present and future are all fixed and determinate. Whatever will be, is; whatever has been, is; whatever is, always has been and always will be. We need not accept the Tralfamadorian view of life to recognize that it represents a commentary on the human lot. For the events of the novel point to a world in which things happen which are beyond our control, in which what we try to control even with the best of intentions often goes awry, and where the forces which shape our destinies are beyond our comprehension even if they are more than simply "the structure of the moment." If the circumstances of existence are thus, then the motto which we are shown once hanging on Billy's wall and once hanging between Montana Wildhack's breasts—"God grant me the serenity to accept the things I cannot change, courage to change the things I can, and wisdom always to tell the difference"—proves ironic to say the least. As the narrator comments: "Among the things Billy Pilgrim could not change were the past, the present, and the future." Or, in other words, accept everything with serenity. Thus the lesson of Tralfamadore has much in common with the admonition to Lot's wife not to look back to Sodom and with Rumfoord's attitude of leaving the history of the Dresden raid as nearly forgotten as possible. It is also implicit in Vonnegut's saying that his book remains a failure because it was written by someone who, like Lot's wife, had been turned into a pillar of salt.

But Kurt Vonnegut looks back. Here the structure of the novel becomes vital to its meaning, for Vonnegut not only looks back to his own Dresden experience but to his previous fiction. If the earlier novels have all been pointing toward Dresden, he now draws arrows back to them, as it were, to connect them with the climactic event. Tracing all of these echoes and repetitions, showing how they unite to produce a cumulative depiction of a world and a pattern of existence emblematized in Dresden and its impact on Billy Pilgrim, would be tedious. The method and effect of the device can be illustrated with a selection of recurrent images, themes, characters or simple incidents.

In the first place, it should be recognized that Billy Pilgrim represents the culmination of a number of traits present in a progressively increasing degree in the earlier protagonists. *Cat's Cradle* makes such generalizations about Vonnegut's protagonists difficult, because its narrator remains something of a non-protagonist. Making allowance for exceptions in that case, however, it becomes possible to deduce some patterns. Each of the protagonists is at least partially a victim of circumstances, either social or cosmic, which effectively control his destiny. The protagonists of the first three novels become captives in a literal way, Jonah and Eliot both undergo confinements, and Billy becomes the prisoner of Germans and Tralfamadorians. Each endures a scene of desolation, from the wrecking of Ilium to the Martian war on Earth to Eliot's imagined firestorm in Indianapolis, leading up to the Dresden conflagration. Faced with the terrors of an absurd, uncontrollable and frequently hostile environment, each is driven toward some form of evasion. As if reality becomes too much to bear, each moves into some kind of unreality or seeming unreality. Emotional disturbance, neurosis, and possible madness emerge in a developing pattern, from Proteus' momentary suspicions of his own mental health to Billy's having himself committed. At least at some point in their lives, all are financially successful men, yet prosperity has little correlation with peace of mind, as the silently weeping optometrist-businessman Billy demonstrates. Most of them have ambivalent feelings toward their fathers which *might* have something to do with their social views but more probably do not. As the prosecutor suggests Proteus' actions express resentment of his father, so Pilgrim's psychiatrist thinks the scares his father has given Billy cause his condition. Both judgments ignore the obvious motivations. But the gulf between father and child parallels that between controlling forces and the man. All follow a literal journey which accompanies the psychological voyage toward awareness. Each is reviled by a society whose moral values are inferior to those it judges warped in the protagonist. Yet each struggles with morality, tries to be a moral man, and evinces an enduring concern to give purpose and goodness to life.

The essential pattern emerges of an unheroic man who is wanderer and prisoner in an absurd universe, a perpetual child dominated by forces he scarce understands, shocked and stunned by incomprehensible horrors, yet somehow finding happiness in moments of joy and love, and doggedly persisting in the effort to be a decent person and to find meaning in existence. Billy epitomizes most of these characteristics. His story may not as fully demonstrate every phase of the pattern as does that of Malachi Constant, but through the war scenes and the central event of Dresden it generates a peculiar force. Dresden becomes the one metaphor around which *Slaughterhouse-Five* builds, like a poem probing the arrested moment and its implications with vivid intensity. (In that respect it might be seen as roughly akin to a poem like Yeats' "Leda and the Swan," building outward or—again the ambiguity—delving inward from its climactic symbolic event, the rape of Leda by Zeus, to the Trojan war and speculations beyond.) By comparison, *The Sirens of Titan* remains more purely narrative in form, demonstrating and explaining its thesis. Billy Pilgrim, wanderer and prisoner on Earth and in space alike, Jesus and Adam, optometrist-businessman and modest loving husband, talk-show crank and preacher of life-in-spite-of-death, traumatized survivor of Dresden, brings together the elements of the pattern in a version of twentieth century combination saint and everyman.

From *Player Piano* comes the setting for the American scenes of *Slaughterhouse-Five:* Ilium, New York. The industrial giant located in Ilium varies from novel to novel, but it remains essentially a one company town. The successive Iliums with their particular resident industries represent the way so many American cities are in fact dominated by one industry or one group of industries—Seattle by Boeing, Detroit by auto manufacturers. But the device goes much further than this, Ilium becoming a representative unit of the larger industrial society, a demonstration-piece for aspects of life under American capitalism. The characteristics developed to an extreme in *Player Piano* recur: domination by a new technological-managerial elite, working masses either being replaced by automation or rendered automatons themselves, people without sense of purpose or self esteem. In Billy's Ilium, the ghetto residents have felt such futility that they have burned down their own neighborhood, making it look like Dresden after being fire-bombed. Nothing could make more explicit the resemblance between what man is doing to man in Ilium and what man did to man in Dresden. Another echo from *Player Piano* comes in images of loneliness, surely an appropriate emotion in the inhabitants of such an environment. One of these images, which occurs several times in Vonnegut's work and twice in *Slaughterhouse-Five*, is of a big dog barking somewhere far off. Each time the sound is the same: "With the help of fear and echoes and winter silences, that dog had a voice like a big bronze gong." We might recall Winston Niles Rumfoord's terrible isolation in being sent finally into endless space without even his dog, Kazak, or the gong-like bark seeming to portend his fate which Constant hears as he enters Rumfoord's estate. Billy hears the gong-bark as he wanders in Luxembourg and as he enters the prison camp—it acts as a signal emphasizing the loneliness of his dual fate as wanderer-prisoner.

From *The Sirens of Titan*, by way of later appearances, come the Rumfoords. Some of the attributes ascribed to this selectively-bred stock in *The Sirens of Titan* seem. both admirable and sincerely intended by Vonnegut. On the other hand, they are typically aloof, somewhat out of touch, lacking in human warmth and compassion. The honeymooning Pilgrims cannot fail to be aware of the passing yacht *Scheherazade*, but on board the honeymooning Lance Rumfoords are a thousand and one nights away from the Pilgrims or anyone like them. The capacities which the Rumfoords have nurtured, which have brought them to power and wealth, are the same ones which allow Bertram Rumfoord to treat both Billy and the story of Dresden so dispassionately or Winston Rumfoord to use people for his own ends with the assurance that his machinations were for their own good. Bertram's insistence that Billy has echolalia demonstrates such attitudes: "Rumfoord was thinking in a military manner: that an inconvenient person, one whose death he wished for very much, for practical reasons, was suffering from a repulsive disease." It is easy to see how he can conclude that Dresden "*had* to be done," and how the Rumfoord approach, subjugating means to ends, individuals to programs, conscience to ambition, will always lead to Dresdens.

Tralfamadore, space and time travel, and visions of a fixed future which negates free will also come from *The Sirens of Titan*. The science fiction element in *Slaughterhouse-Five* shares the basic ingredients it provides in other novels: an outside perspective on human affairs; a means of projecting the mundane to bizarre extremes which expose its characteristics by exaggeration; a literal "universalizing" of given conditions. Billy's journey to Tralfamadore and his being placed in a zoo there act in part as parallels to his wanderings in Luxembourg and his internment in the German camp, emphasizing that the war experiences are not unique ones dependent upon particular circumstances but are emblematic of the general condition of man in the cosmos. The Tralfamadorian insistence that things happen simply because that is "the way the moment was structured" and that people in time are like insects trapped in a blob of amber also emphasizes the condition of man in broad existential terms. The space story provides a context for the war episodes. Picked up by the Tralfamadorians, Billy's only question is, "Why me?" His captors explain that there is no *why*—it just is. Soon afterwards, in the counterpointed narrative of the German prisoners, an American is unexpectedly struck by a guard. "Why me?" he asks. "'Vy you? Vy anybody?'" responds the guard. In short, the story of Billy's capture and of Dresden, with its insistent *whys* and its persistent absurd inevitability provides the perfect embodiment of the vision of existence which the Tralfamadorian episodes in Vonnegut diagram.

There is another aspect of the science fiction, also pervasive in *The Sirens of Titan*, which calls attention to itself in *Slaughterhouse-Five*. That is the element of evasion or escape. For while the science fiction stresses grim aspects of existence—inevitability, meaninglessness, alienation and isolation, the absurd—it remains itself an escape into imagination and fancy. This ambivalence of science fiction contributes to the mixed tone common in Vonnegut, strongest in *The Sirens of Titan* but considerable in this novel, of cutting satirical exposure balanced by wistful expression of tenderness, of harsh visions of the existential void mingled with lingering glimpses of a warmer world. At the same time that Billy's space journey extends the existential terms of his earthly journey, it also contains some of the happiest, most comforting moments of his life. The Tralfamadorians themselves seem kind, and apparently do their best to treat Billy with understanding. He feels as happy there as on earth, his little zoo world seems cozy, and his relationship with Montana Wildhack is a loving one. In fact, it looks almost like erotic dream come true combined with ideal matrimonial harmony, the sweet innocence of Adam and Eve recreated in the snug safety of a geodesic Eden. And while the Tralfamadorians confirm his experience of inevitable subjection to incomprehensible forces, they also provide him with an answer. The perpetual existence of all moments of time removes the negation of death. As surely as man dies man is always alive in those moments that he lived. That is the vision that Billy preaches in the final years of his life and which enables him to face the death he has foreseen without fear or regret.

If in these respects the time and space travel looks like wish-fulfillment or escape from reality, that is entirely appropriate. We must surely wonder, like his daughter and others in the novel, if all Billy's talk of Tralfamadore and time travel is not madness. When Billy commits himself he shares his room with Eliot Rosewater. Eliot has killed a fourteen-year-old German fireman and Billy has seen "the greatest massacre in European history," and both find life meaningless. "So they were trying to re-invent themselves and their universe. Science fiction was a big help." That comment could suggest that all the time and space travels are tricks of Billy's mind, "oubliettes" into which it escapes as the only way to make life bearable. The first time Billy "flips out" he is exhausted, cold, hungry, scared and in pain: hallucinatory escape from reality in such circumstances seems completely plausible. Subsequently there are interconnections between "reality" and the time travel which help suggest the latter could be dreams or hallucinations derived from the former. The idea of a man and woman being kidnapped by space men and displayed in a zoo occurs in a Kilgore Trout novel Billy reads. Orange and black stripes appear on the locomotive of the POW train, on the tent used for daughter Barbara's wedding reception, and on the moonlit hall wall as Billy walks to the flying saucer. Some room remains for lingering suspicions that all the science fiction elements exist only in Billy's mind (as the Indianapolis conflagration exists only in Eliot's mind in *God Bless You, Mr. Rosewater*), even though the story is told as if they were factual. That would not diminish their impact or their service to theme, and it would even intensify the poignancy of the sufferings inflicted on Billy by his experience. Nor does the possible ambiguity weaken the story. As with the moral uncertainties surrounding Campbell's confessions in *Mother Night*, we have it both ways, in effect, so that the range of psychological and thematic exploration is broadened.

The science fiction technique, then, dramatizes the general condition of man in an Absurd Universe captured metaphorically and literally in the Dresden episode, and expresses the inevitable desire to escape at least momentarily from such a vision of reality. *Mother Night* showed the same wartime nightmare and the same wish for evasion. The connection with that novel comes partly through the general images of human suffering in wartime, partly through the similar depiction of the rights and wrongs of both sides in the war, and through the character of Howard Campbell. In most respects, the Campbell of *Slaughterhouse-Five* seems consistent with the one seen in *Mother Night*, though curiously one detail does not fit—this time he is married to *Resi* Noth, not Helga. Another detail carried over from the same novel is the "Blue Fairy Godmother." In *Mother Night* that was Campbell's name for the American intelligence officer who recruited him. This time it is the appellation for a British prisoner, deriving from the role he plays in the welcoming pantomime. Campbell's main function consists of commenting on the nature of American prisoners in general, tracing their behavior to the influence of their native class system. That system is described in terms resembling those declared in *God Bless You, Mr. Rosewater*. The American enlisted men, Campbell says, despise themselves because they see their poverty as a sign of their own failure. They love neither themselves nor one another, reject any leadership from among their ranks as pretension by someone no better than they are, and therefore make sulky, self-pitying prisoners. If the portrayal of men as prisoners of war is seen as a metaphor for the general condition of man, then the consequences of the system decried in *God Bless You, Mr. Rosewater* are shown in *Slaughterhouse-Five* not just for what they do to Americans as soldiers and prisoners but for their larger human cost.

Other repetitions abound. Those references to writing about days of catastrophe and to the Children's Crusade from *Cat's Cradle* have already been mentioned. As in that book, there is talk here of fabrication being necessary to explain life, when Eliot Rosewater tells a psychiatrist, "'I think you guys are going to have to come up with a lot of wonderful *new* lies, or people just aren't going to want to go on living.'" The frightening incomprehensibility which demands lies in *Cat's Cradle* is intensified in the senseless horror of Dresden. Well might the questioning bird call, surely an existential "Why?" which punctuates other novels as it does this one, provide the last word—"*Poo-tee-weet?*"

In sum, the allusions to other novels serve to enlarge and complete the significance of the central action of *Slaughterhouse-Five*, while this novel in turn draws together what has been shown in the earlier ones. It also gathers the multiple episodes of its own story into its main symbolic event. All the contemporary events depicted—ghetto riot, Vietnam war, assassinations of Martin Luther King and Robert F. Kennedy—become part of the existential absurdity crystallized in the firebombing of Dresden. Everything is united in a consistent, concise vision of the world according to Vonnegut. That vision remains descriptive more than interpretive, but the carefully assembled events speak vividly and the moral imperatives emerge with force. The structural technique employed in *Slaughterhouse-Five* gives a short novel depth, complexity and inclusiveness, all delivered with an impact intensified by compression.

Having shown us the hideous reality and the universal ramifications of the destruction of Dresden, what does Vonnegut offer us with which to meet such a world? On the face of it, very little. The general implications of this story might be that war and hate and various forms of cruelty are bad. There is nothing new in that, although the force with which these stock observations are made does revitalize their horror and perhaps reinvigorate our conviction that such things must cease. As the movie producer says to the author on hearing he has written an anti-war novel, "'Why don't you write an anti-*glacier* book instead?'" Perhaps Vonnegut accepts the challenge in extending *Slaughterhouse-Five* into more than an anti-war novel. The pens of anti-war writers may never be mightier than swords, and the voices of men crying out against the absurdity of existence may echo away in the recesses of unheeding space, but there is morality and humanity in man's making the effort. As Vonnegut says of Lot's wife, he loves her for looking back because it was such a human thing to do. Vonnegut looks back, and the result is a very human book. Both of them, he says, are turned into pillars of salt. The implication seems to be that to look back at such a catastrophe, at so much human suffering, is to become immobilized by sorrow, to be so caught up in the horror and grief of what life has brought as to be unable to go on living. That might be what is meant by Billy Pilgrim's becoming "unstuck in time." Shocked by his experience, trapped in the memory of horrors, he cannot go on living moment by consecutive moment. At this point the quotations Vonnegut uses in the first chapter become relevant. The first is from Theodore Roethke's "The Waking":

> I wake to sleep, and take my waking slow.
> I feel my fate in what I cannot fear.
> I learn by going where I have to go.

The sleep he wakes to is surely death, which, along with the pains of life, is what he cannot fear and also the event toward which he has to go. The other two quotations express, first, the view that life is a dance with death, and second, the wish to stop the action of life so that it will not come to an end. What these quotations seem to add up to is the view that life is "a duty dance with death," an inevitable course leading to an inevitable end. To fear either life or death, to be immobilized by fright or horror or grief, means to give up living and become a pillar of salt.

We might conclude from this that Vonnegut advocates acceptance of the unchangeable course of life and of death itself, not looking back, enjoying the dance and the good moments life brings. As he says, "People aren't supposed to look back." But they do, and that they do is human and lovable. That undercuts the apparent assertion about the way life should be lived, as does the fact that it so closely resembles the system, derisively portrayed, by which the Tralfamadorians shut their eyes to the bad moments and travel in the times of happiness. Vonnegut speaks in the final chapter of being glad to have so many nice moments in his life, but there are not many offered in *Slaughterhouse-Five*. The one he mentions, of flying over East Germany in a Hungarian airplane, is punctuated with thoughts of bombings and the world's overpopulation, and set between accounts of political assassinations, Vietnam death tolls and Dresden corpse mines. As the novel ends, Billy is enjoying a happier moment in springtime sunshine, but the coffin-shaped wagon stands nearby and the bird overhead repeats the questioning *"Poo-tee-weet?"* The ambiguities persist to the end.

In general terms, however, the advocacy of keeping going, avoiding becoming unstuck in time through obsession with the painful past, and making the most of the happy moments, seems to be endorsed through the presentation of the British POWs. They are also undercut: the error which gives them five hundred Red Cross parcels a month instead of fifty detracts from the notion that they have succeeded entirely by their own efforts, and the German commandant's anglophiliac admiration of them adds to the touch of parody in their description. Yet the tribute paid them in the novel seems as genuinely intended as the criticism of the American prisoners, and the merits of their approach in contrast to that of their allies stand. For five years they have kept going in circumstances which, parcels or no parcels, remain demoralizing, and, more than that, they have given meaning and purpose to an existence as absurd as any imaginable. Perhaps through them we are shown the value of giving life purpose and making happiness rather than constantly turning away to ask, "Why me?" "Do I feel happy?" or "What does life mean?" Their system works better than anything else we see in the novel. And yet, finally, we are left feeling it does not really carry much weight. Vonnegut stops well short of offering us a program for life, as if afraid that if he does he, too, might be guilty of giving us a set of lies which make life tolerable. In fact, there is far less affirmation in this novel than in

The Sirens of Titan. There are indications of values placed on compassion, uncritical love and the joy of living, but they seem pallid and weak in this context of nightmare. We are left with the stillness following the disaster, the vague promise of that tired, faded spring light, and the bird's eternal "*Poo-tee-weet?*"

Yet *Slaughterhouse-Five* is not a humorless book. It has its full measure of the usual delightful satiric barbs, slapstick scenes and comic preposterousness. The account of the drunk Billy searching desperately for the steering wheel of his car not knowing that he is in the back seat evokes laughter but seems like something we have seen before. Billy's coming unstuck in time while watching television, so that he sees a war film backwards then forwards is funny, satirically sharp, and thematically to the point. But much of the humor remains dark or even embittered. Typical is the repetition of the Tralfamadorian "So it goes" after each mention of death. The repeated phrase becomes something like an incremental refrain, building meaning with each restatement. At first it seems funny in an ironic way, then it begins to sound irritating, almost irreverent. Gradually we realize that our irritation is right, that the punctuating refrain is forcing us to look at another then another death, and we are won over to the device, our resentment now directed to the fact which it emphasizes, that too many people are killed. "So it goes," initially almost a shrugging acceptance of the inevitable, becomes a grim reminder meaning almost the opposite of what it says, and finally another more poignant kind of expression of the inevitable. By the last chapter, when it is applied to the deaths of Robert Kennedy, Martin Luther King, and young men in Vietnam, the device which had first brought smiles leaves us close to tears. And so it goes.

In the first chapter, Vonnegut calls *Slaughterhouse-Five* a failure. We can understand why he might think so, since it is so evidently an attempt to capture the full measure of such a personally significant event and perhaps even a great deal of what he believes about life in general. Few men are likely to finish such an effort feeling they have said it all or said it right. He might also feel that technically the novel has inadequacies. It does. Some of them, such as in characterization, have been mentioned. Yet overall *Slaughterhouse-Five* remains a remarkably successful novel, and in some ways Vonnegut's best. It shows less of the warm humanity which we come to feel is part of Vonnegut's vision of life than we might hope for and than we find in *The Sirens of Titan*. It also finds less to affirm, too. But *Slaughterhouse-Five* is an enormously truthful book, and truth in this case leaves little room for faith or assurance that is the least bit forced. The novel flirts with the dangers of being episodic, disjointed, too diverse, and even too brief, for its content. In this respect it is a daring novel, but that artistic recklessness pays off. The structure does hold, and succeeds in pulling together not just its own components but ideas and themes from previous novels. And all without turning the book into a compendium. The compression gives a story which could become turgid vitality, yet at the same time intensifies its poignancy. Moreover, the novel neither falters from, nor sensationalizes the horrors it depicts, and tenaciously avoids pedantic or moralistic commentary; no small achievement given the subject matter and the author's personal closeness to it.

PETER G. JONES

At War with Technology: Kurt Vonnegut, Jr.

Kurt Vonnegut's work displays uniquely the thematic fusion of technology (or science) and war. Both elements dominate: war consistently demands spectacular new achievements from science; and technology flourishes in the hothouse of conflict. In addition, war provides an immediate focus for all the ingenuity that science and "progerse" can muster. Finally, in a special way synonymous with science and the idea of progress, war provides a milieu particularly suited to Vonnegut's depictions of modern life.

Several common denominators link his novels. Vonnegut sneers at the concept of free will, a delusion found in all the universe only among the dominant fauna of the planet Earth, according to the observations of Tralfamadorian passers-by. He bemoans the "stupidity and viciousness" of humanity, delineates the infinite variety of human duplicity—and, for the record, refuses to take anything seriously. Identity-enigmas proliferate almost as freely as his intentional misquotations and fractured allusions. And there is a consistent inconsistency in details from book to book: a Heraclitean flux alters the perspective, characters, and historical incidents with each retelling. Vonnegut's first novel raises the theme basic to the rest: in the last battle, man will fight his own technology for survival. *Player Piano* (published in 1952) is a clear call to arms, sounded early in the campaign. By the 1970s American fiction and nonfiction alike reflected a similar, growing

From *War and the Novelist: Appraising the American War Novel.* © 1976 by the Curators of the University of Missouri.

dissatisfaction with rationalism. The player piano that figures in the novel demonstrates the uneasy alliance of art and science, showing technology's fatal influence on the human spirit. The player piano is but another facet of the same science that replaces men with computers to make Earth "an engineer's paradise."

Paul Proteus and his father prefigure Dr. Hoenikker, who brings the final blessing of science in *Cat's Cradle*. Hoenikker's stray Labrador and Paul's cat represent links with the vital natural world: both are destroyed. The dog is Ice-Nine's first victim; the cat is incinerated by the automated janitorial and security systems of Proteus's engineering works, located in that part of New York where Proteus Steinmetz worked earlier, shaping the twentieth century. Paul's father has organized and automated the science of his country in its defense. Now Paul is heir apparent, with emotions like those that fill Julian Castle of *Cat's Cradle* when first presented with his father's legacy of corpses.

A full generation before the space age forced science to yield the full bounty of technological miracles, Vonnegut fired this warning salvo. Paul Proteus is tried for betraying his trust, for plotting to limit the scope of machines in the lives of the American people. To do so, he insists, is right: "A step backward, after making a wrong turn, is a step in the right direction." Earlier he had dared ask whether it might be possible to do something wrong in the name of progress. With Priest Lasher and latter-day Sinn Fein Finnerty, he recklessly tries to turn the nation around. Their movement is called the Ghost Shirts, echoing an earlier similarly futile attempt by the American Indians to resist "progerse." All people except the managers are, in Vonnegut's vision, like the beleaguered and betrayed Indians of *Bury My Heart at Wounded Knee*.

Though *Slaughterhouse-Five* is Vonnegut's most widely known work, *Cat's Cradle* is in many respects more intriguing. It is an independent work, whereas *Slaughterhouse-Five* draws heavily on *Sirens of Titan*; *God Bless You, Mr. Rosewater*; and *Mother Night*. These form a preliminary triptych, providing collectively a seedbed for the characterizations and ideas of *Slaughterhouse-Five*.

Sirens of Titan (published in 1959) shows that creation, as Genesis describes it, was merely an intricate process for providing a critical spare part for Salo, the errant Tralfamadorian messenger, stranded on Titan. Destined to spend millennia there, Salo cannot continue his appointed rounds until Space Wanderer, formerly Unk, born Malachi Constant, "happens" along. Married now to the former wife of god-like Rumfoord and father to a semiwild son, the Wanderer unwittingly supplies the vital piece for Salo's C+ inter-galactic space-phaeton (as in $E=MC^2$).

Deism is a strong and early theme in Vonnegut's novels. Eons since, machines gladly replaced the moribund vertebrates of Tralfamadore and now continue the mission of greeting the far corners of the universe. Later, in *Cat's Cradle*, Bokonian Genesis records the moment when Adam, still groggily half-baked, sits up, stares about in puzzlement, and wonders about the purpose of "all this." God asks, "Everything must have a purpose?"—and departs, a bit confused himself. He leaves his great machine, in Conrad's phrase, "to knit when it should embroider."

As in the short stories, even this early novel segues firmly away from science fiction as a sufficient theme, to fiction that uses science mainly for immediate background. Frustration, problems of identity, and a dominant Vonnegut theme—that people are continually used for ends they themselves know nothing of—these weave the pattern of *Sirens*. Ultimately God toys with all of humanity, and to no particular end. This God is remarkably like Professor Hoenikker of *Cat's Cradle*. He is a technician so fascinated by the infinite possibilities of process that he cares nothing for consequences. This realization brings Bokonon to the point of freezing himself with Ice-Nine, creating a recumbent statue, eternally thumbing his nose at "You Know Who."

In *Sirens*, Malachi Constant is the playboy of Earth. Outrageously rich and equally immoral, he is lobotomized by Niles Rumfoord and sent on his special mission. Rumfoord's "chance" venture into the interstitial labyrinth of the space warp's "chrono-synclastically infundibulated" Never-Never Land places him in a position directly analogous to Constant's, but at a higher level. Like Billy Pilgrim of *Slaughterhouse-Five*, Niles is an inveterate time traveler. Unlike Billy he has some vague idea of the general purpose and a schedule of sorts, an arrangement which allows him to materialize for brief periods at his home on Earth. Also Niles Rumfoord has a sense of mission; unfortunately, the wrong mission. God is to Rumfoord as Rumfoord is to Constant. And so it goes. In *Cat's Cradle* Hoenikkers's elder son, Frank, places various combinations of bugs in a bottle and watches them fight. Then, just as on that day near Alamagordo and on the day Hiroshima died, Hoenikker, too, thought he knew what he was doing—thought himself the master of a process whose ultimate end is totally beyond him.

Niles uses Malachi in his great invasion of Earth, a later elaboration on the tempestuous family reunion staged at Hastings in 1066. The "Martians" are in fact Earth people who have been kidnapped to Mars, conditioned, and launched homeward in suicidal disarray with hopelessly antiquated weapons to bring to fruition Rumfoord's grand design for Earth. Because he moves with relative freedom in time Niles thinks himself a veritable god. But though he knows the future, he still thinks it possible to change events. He capitalizes on the invasion to establish a new religion and to make of this

particular war something truly useful and therefore memorable. Setting the
stage for the new religion, this war will be cost-effective. A "magnificently
led few will . . . die for a great deal," rather than allowing millions to pass
beneath the "quick lid" of Earth for Mom, apple pie, and Vaterland. Like
others before him, however, Mr. Rumfoord is deceived. A dupe, he tries to
improve things through war.

The rule of necessity is unsubtly present. Malachi Constant (constant
messenger) seems invulnerable in his wealth and overwhelming immorality.
But he becomes an automaton, dumbly bound by the destiny once recited for
his edification. Earth to Mars to Mercury to Earth to Titan—and he is done.
No. Unknown to him, the final stop is Earth. The immediate director of
Mars's demise, Rumfoord thinks that because he knows some he knows all.
But near the novel's end, on Titan, as his faithful dog fades into a fissure in
the continuum of Time, and he himself slides helplessly elsewhere, Niles is
forced to the realization that he is but another dupe, of Whom? Earlier he
explained for Chrono (and the reader) the meaning of human history, and
the meaning of the Constant family motto: "The messenger awaits." Even
mechanical Salo revolted, committing suicide after revealing his message to
Rumfoord. But "as it was supposed to happen," Malachi reassembled him,
and Salo's sense of mission returns.

Sirens of Titan introduces the first of Vonnegut's long series of womb
images—here, the Cave of Harmoniums on Mercury. Feeding on the music
of their sphere, the Harmoniums are exquisite parasites, displaying at once
the beauty, utter harmlessness, and essential futility of art. The failures of art
incite the rage of Eliot Rosewater in *God Bless You, Mr. Rosewater*. Similarly
in *Cat's Cradle* art somehow fails to redeem the world from the curse of
science, despite Angela's noble suicide and Newt's enigmatic paintings. In
Mother Night Howard Campbell and his Russian friend are practicing artists
(playwright and painter, respectively) whose work ornaments their lives but
does not deter its ultimately negative course. Art fails because this universe
is the grand design of a bumbling mechanic. It has no purpose but to run,
and it makes no provision for esthetics.

Niles Rumfoord is the presiding vicar of destiny in Sirens. Another
Rumfoord appears in *Slaughterhouse-Five*. Sharing Billy Pilgrim's hospital
room, this "Harvard history professor, Brigadier General in the Air Force
Reserve, official Air Force historian, author of twenty-six books, and a
multimillionaire since birth," represents, as Niles does in *Titan*, the worst
possible elements of applied "progerse." Whereas Niles Rumfoord is
"chrono-synclastically infundibulated," Billy P. is merely unstuck in time.
Rumfoord appears to know what is going on, although that appearance is
deceptive; Billy is simply dumbfounded by events. The change to a simpler

terminology and to a less complex protagonist in this later book points up Vonnegut's altered focus. Perhaps convinced that issues are more complicated than he thought, Vonnegut presents a more open plot, not closed out, as in the earlier novels, with the neatness of suicidal vow, satirical mimicry of biblical injunction, smugly neat death of exploited messenger, or impending martyrdom of mod messiah. *Slaughterhouse-Five* ends only twenty-three years after it began, more than twenty years before the wavering cross-hairs on the sights of Lazzaro's laser come to rest on the expectant speaker in Chicago. Here, time really is out of joint, and perhaps not even He Who started it all can make it right. Vonnegut might be demonstrating that though death comes to all, it may not solve anything. The author no longer flaunts his mastery of events; the center of attention is beleaguered Man, Billy Pilgrim.

As the author generously explains in a later edition, the title of his novel, *Mother Night*, is taken from a speech by Mephistopheles in *Faust*, wherein Goethe's devil proclaims the primacy of Darkness and the inevitability of its triumph. So it is in this novel. As Mephisto is used and toyed with by God, so Howard Campbell is exploited. Young Campbell is recently married to a German beauty, launched upon a life of fulfillment as poet and playwright. But an unprepossessing agent of his government recruits Campbell on the eve of World War II. A combination of Lord Haw Haw and Ezra Pound, Campbell broadcasts nightly vituperation of the U.S.A. as he is bid by the Nazi regime. His efforts earn him the hate of his homeland, grateful admiration from the Nazis, and dutiful respect from the officer who hired him and from President Roosevelt—the only two persons aware of his role. Campbell's nocturnal blasts carry coded information through the ether. After the war he is captured by a zealous young American officer and tried, then released on a technicality. The official gratitude of his nation does not include recognition, so he is literally smuggled back home and allowed to live in seclusion.

Campbell is sought out for various reasons by diverse elements of his public. The Israelis classify him with Eichmann. When he finally surrenders to their agents, he winds up in a cell next to that worthy. Here the story begins—and ends. These edited memoirs, complete with the editor's protestations, reveal the harsh and crabbed course that destiny allotted for Campbell. The Russians want Campbell as an exhibit to show the world what kind of reprehensible beings the U.S. shelters from justice. Ex-Lieutenant O'Hare, who captured Campbell, wants to finish the job that was interrupted before at the scaffold steps. To the American Nazi party in its sick mutations, Campbell is a hero, sought out as patron saint and cosmic celebrity. And the FBI is interested because of the weird human congeries that swirl about him.

Mother Night (published in 1961) sets the moral and philosophical tone for the rest of Vonnegut's novels (with the exception of Eliot Rosewater's benign ". . . be fruitful and multiply," which concludes that book). It's all here: Mother Night is the presiding power, and with some humor. The blatant Russian plagiarist who finds the trunk concealing Campbell's literary masterpieces proves to be smashingly successful with the poems and plays, until the regime finds that he has unleashed a deadly intellectual virus: he is shot for displaying originality. Identities slip and slide: Campbell himself was a double agent; a genial middle-aged artist who is Campbell's neighbor during his years of hiding proves to be a Russian spy (shades of Colonel Abel); when Campbell's dead German wife miraculously reappears, she proves to be the woman's younger sister, also a Russian spy; and Colonel Frank Wirtanen, who recruited Campbell for his wartime role surfaces in a letter to the imprisoned Campbell. Now named Sparrow, he offers to testify at Campbell's impending trial. Campbell refers to Wirtanen as his "Blue Fairy Godmother," a term carried over into *Slaughterhouse-Five* and applied to a particularly efficient and compassionate British prisoner of war. O'Hare also appears in *Slaughterhouse-Five*, as the anonymous narrator's wartime companion.

Suicide appears prominently in Vonnegut's books. Whether this is stoicism, existentialism, or merely an unconscious device, he uses it consistently. Beginning here in *Mother Night*, it is a topic always near at hand. When Resi Noth, masquerading as the lost wife, Helga, dabs her lips to deposit cyanide there, the reader sees the planting of an idea that blooms into glorious harvest in *Cat's Cradle*, where the Ice-Nine statue-making business claims tens of thousands. In particular, Resi prefaces the mocking suicide of Mona. Eliot Rosewater wanders along the brink of suicide, trying to forget the young firemen he killed in the war. One of the Rosewater uncles hangs himself to solve a financial dilemma. And in *Cat's Cradle* the theme is fully developed. Suicide is indeed the single irreversible and catastrophic act that a man can perform totally of his own will, defying even God. As the Bokonian rules for the game specify, the act is preceded by the triumphant incantation: "Now I will destroy the whole world."

In *Mother Night* war is everywhere. Campbell is able to sustain himself for a generation on war surplus items. Racism, espionage, and political chicanery all reflect the temper of these times. Campbell recounts war's minor horrors, including the death by hanging of his father-in-law, recalls anecdotes accumulated during his acquaintance with the Eichmann syndrome in captivity, and the passionate pronouncements of the American Nazis. He offers this analogy for the condition of the soul "in a man at war": it is like "the stink, diseased twilight, humid resonance, and vile privacy of a stall in a public lavatory."

The narrator of *Mother Night* looks for death as a relief from a world in which "a human being might as well look for diamond tiaras in the gutter as for rewards and punishments that [are] fair." Self-taught about God, Campbell expects nothing from "Him." Tired of attempting to solve the complexities of causes and effects that do not match, Campbell surrenders to the Israelis and looks forward to the suicide that will soon end his problems, foiling Colonel Wirtanen's generous gesture.

The problem with Eliot Rosewater of *God Bless You, Mr. Rosewater* (published in 1965) is that while fighting in World War II with his infantry unit and exhibiting his usual exemplary military prowess, he inadvertently kills some German firemen, mistaking their uniforms for those of soldiers. After the war he becomes an alcoholic, marries a beautiful woman, inherits the staggering wealth of the Rosewater foundation, starts a life-long career of underwriting firemen and fire-fighting units, and becomes an authentic practicing philanthropist.

After wandering for years, he realizes that his conscience cannot be outdistanced, so he settles down in the Rosewater Vaterland (Indiana) to do good among the people. Howard Campbell had his "ratty attic" in Greenwich Village. In *Cat's Cradle* the oubliette that the narrator and the other survivors of Ice-Nine share is more tomb than womb: an underground hide-away that could easily become their final resting place. Eliot's refuge is a smaller cubicle, though complete with toilet and telephone. As is typical of Vonnegut, this image is evoked in the mangled Freudianism of Dr. Brown's treatise on civilization and conscience. With the population at large, the battle between enlightened self-interest and conscience has reached such proportions that "a normal person, functioning well on the upper levels of a prosperous, industrialized society, can hardly hear his conscience at all." From the remainder of the treatise, the reader quickly learns that Eliot's disease is not alcoholism, but simply the obsessive, persistent desire to love and to want to help others. Eliot is virtually unique in his affliction. Wife Sylvia is more nearly normal. Reacting to his unstinting compassion toward the great unwashed, she lapses into "samaritrophia," which is "hysterical indifference to the troubles of those less fortunate than oneself." The special "oubliette" of *God Bless You, Mr. Rosewater* is psychological, the hole into "the tyrannous conscience" is pitched by "the rest of the mind" in the final development of maturing samaritrophia. Precisely because he is so humanely involved with other people, Eliot has, according to the learned Dr. Brown, a terrible potential for the disease. But Eliot prevails, a personification of that overwhelmed but undaunted conscience.

Norman Mushari is sick with envy of Rosewater, and determined to help a feckless cousin disinherit Eliot. Norman's adolescent trivium was building model airplanes, masturbating, and admiring the power of Senator Joe McCarthy. His psyche suggests the later statue, created on the plains of Titan by Salo, of the genius who discovered atomic power, displayed in the mechanical Tralfamadorian's stone impression "with a shocking erection." Eliot is a gentle man, mad with love for others. As in *Slaughterhouse-Five*, he is fond of William Blake, whose poetry expresses Eliot's feelings and adorns the otherwise unmemorable interior of his cell. Mushari's conniving comes to naught when Eliot recovers his "sanity" and is able to take control of the Rosewater fortunes.

Into *God Bless You, Mr. Rosewater* Vonnegut crams most of the traditional devices of the novel, dating from the epistolary tradition onward through the myriad recognitions, mysterious documents, and unusual events that unfold during the course of an English novel. A key element is Dr. Brown's report on the Rosewaters—one source of Mushari's scheme. In addition, there are Eliot's mad-Hamlet letters to Sylvia, Senator Rosewater's speeches on the merits of free enterprise, Harvey Ulm's paranoid fugitive poetry and his novel, the famous Rosewater family history, and the philosophy of Kilgore Trout. But, whereas John Barth uses such traditional material to reproduce the aura of the learned eighteenth-century author, as in *The Sot Weed Factor*, and to create an intricately wrought plot, as in *Giles Goat Boy*, Vonnegut strews his building blocks with apparent abandon, perhaps striving for the hidden architectonic of Dos Passos's *Manhattan Transfer* or of James Joyce's *Ulysses*. Perhaps.

But among jumbled shards such as Ulm's Mailer-esque celebration of the "old avenger," the Rosewater genealogy, and Eliot's poetic madness, the Vonnegut themes come through insistently. An example is Eliot's version of Plato's myth of Er from the *Republic*. Plato explains that souls waiting to be reborn must return to Earth as a matter of expiation. They do not choose wisely because they are, after all, fallibly human. In Eliot's version, "Heaven is an utter bore." Souls famished for the experience of space and time take whatever life is offered them by the Master Cynic, God. The narrator notes, however, that something in the quality of twentieth-century life is causing newly eligible souls to swear off reincarnation. Somehow, life now is worse than during periods when inquisitions and other consequences of superstitions made earthly life a truly active hell.

Kilgore Trout emerges as something of a philosopher, an adviser to Senator Rosewater. Prolific with ideas but totally without promise as a writer, Trout earlier elicits Eliot's anguished lament that his ideas go unacknowledged because nobody will wade through the unforgivable prose that drowns them. Trout explains the Protestant ethic, as further elaborated by Emerson, to the senator: "Americans have long been taught to hate all people who will not or cannot work, to hate even themselves for that." Eliot's work in Rosewater country was a noble experiment in "how to love people who have no use." In time, Trout reasons, progress will make all people useless—a notion that explains the indifference of the deistic God who inhabits Vonnegut's pages. Trout also points out the non-Freudian explanation for Eliot's obsession with firefighters and their departments. The volunteer fire department represents the only consistent practice of "enthusiastic unselfishness" in contemporary American life. So neither the insanity that Mushari hoped to reveal nor the massive guilt complex that to the unsubtle reader seems obvious is, in fact, the true explanation.

God Bless You, Mr. Rosewater is a prime example of the time-warp, kitchen-midden school of writing. In anticipation of *Slaughterhouse-Five, God Bless You* introduces a book about the bombing of Dresden. Reading it, Eliot is visited by a vision of the world's demise, made real to him by a vision of Indianapolis, fire-bombed. There is also this image of myth and history, art and carnality, interleaved: the picture of the Shetland pony and two whores, one of whom is about to try an "impossible sexual congress." The Rosewater family tree is joined to that of the Rumfoords, and a small bird utters in explication: "Poo-tee-weet?" as Eliot emerges from the dark night of his apocalyptic vision. Strongly attracted by it, Eliot explores the dry fountain in Dr. Brown's garden, suggesting Malachi Constant's entrance to the Rumfoord estate in *Sirens of Titan*, and of course Constant's subsequent problems with mental health, stability, and identity. A Trout novel, picked up at random by Eliot, again introduces the Tralfamadorians and the end. Not the end of the world, but the death of "the Milky Way." That's the way it goes when chrono-synclastic infundibulation sets in.

Cat's Cradle (published in 1963) is about a scientist who read "nothing," was fascinated by processes, asked "What is sin?"—and found a way to end the world: Ice-Nine. Perhaps inspired by Frost's nine-line poem on the subject, Vonnegut shows one way that the unthinking, dispassionate curiosity of positivist science could end the world in the twentieth century, just incidentally, while employed in the service of technological war. Frost's poem suggests the treacherous hatred of Dante's ninth circle; it is in polar opposition to the heat of desire. In Vonnegut's world all emotion is dead, and the key word might be indifference. Disinterested science, dead to moral responsibility and indifferent to the implications of the processes it develops, perpetrates monumental, indeed, the ultimate, fraud.

In *Pentagon of Power* (the title ingeniously fuses the symbol for twentieth-century power with the traditional symbol for the dark metaphysics of magic), Lewis Mumford suggests that for the Faustian mind of this century there is a new categorical imperative: "If it can be done, it must be done." This same theme crops up in Erich Fromm's surprising *Anatomy of Human Destructiveness*. So it is with Vonnegut's scientist, Hoenikker, who is chillingly unlike Dr. Oppenheimer in whose image he appears to have been conceived. Whereas Dr. Oppenheimer reportedly sought refuge in the Bhagavad-Gita on the awesome morning in Yucca Flat, Dr. Hoenikker "plays" cat's cradle with his terrified son on the day that Hiroshima is blasted.

Hoenikker is an archetypal positivist. His simple faith is that he recovers "truth" by experimentation; that the more truth science reveals, the wealthier and better the world will be. Outwardly mild-mannered and inoffensive, Hoenikker relates the pyramidal stacks of cannon balls on courthouse lawns to the molecular models that form the matrix of his own enterprises. He smelled, his son recalls, "like the mouth of Hell." To his immediate supervisor, Hoenikker was a force of nature, but he himself observes with scientific superiority that though nature was competent to create Ice-One, it was for man to create Ice-Nine. Hoenikker is unconcerned with morals. Vonnegut places the obvious rejoinder in the mouth of a nonscientific observer: "How innocent is the man who made the bomb?" Having created both fire and ice sufficient to effect the world's end, Hoenikker is content merely to let fate decide which it will be. Vonnegut brings to bay the public morality of the twentieth century; here he evokes the sharp memory of Dr. Oppenheimer, charged by his country with the task of unlocking the atom's eschatological secret, then rebuked and censured for shrinking from the consequences of exploiting his awful vision.

The story line of *Cat's Cradle* is relatively simple, incorporating themes by now de rigueur in Vonnegut's Gothic fiction: lost manuscripts, apocryphal histories, protean characters, an unidentified narrator, a dominant strain of war, and a foretaste of the end of the world. The narrator looks for Hoenikker's children, seeking information for his own book now in progress. With his dog, Hoenikker is the first to taste the fruits of Ice-Nine, leaving a legacy sufficient to enable the world to follow in his frosty steps. Hoenikker evokes the memory of Rumfoord and his dog, Kazak. Rumfoord also sought to improve things, and thought he knew best. Hoenikker's children are Angela, the angular and unlovely clarinetist, Newton, the gnomish painter, and Frank, whose profession is architecture, encompassing both science and art in a questionable relationship. The search leads to Ilium, New York, and then to San Lorenzo. Directing the affairs of San Lorenzo's beloved dictator, Papa, Frank brings about disaster. Papa outlawed religion, that it may flourish and give the people hope in their misery. Felled by Big C., Papa opts out with Ice-Nine in a small personal suicide that is unfortunately complicated by a predestined and therefore necessary "accident."

Mr. Vonnegut's obsessive reflections on the predestinarian nature of the universe permeate this book, too. The narrator notes that events occur "as they are supposed to happen." A prelude to the arresting "bugs in amber" metaphor of *Slaughterhouse-Five* occurs in *Cat's Cradle* when Angela produces a family picture, images "trapped in plexiglas." Some of Vonnegut's devices, however, are almost unforgivable: the narrator is saved from death because he steps stage left to vomit the large part of his rich meal—an albatross shot from the very battlements of Castle San Lorenzo; preparing to play her clarinet, Angela's fingers "twittered idly over the noiseless keys"; on the day of the first atomic detonation, when a colleague remarks that science has now known sin, Dr. Hoenikker replies, "What is sin?"; in San Lorenzo, virtually the only capital offense involves playing footsie, literally; and, asked if people still die on the antique barbed device of execution that is one of the country's chief attractions, a native responds, "It's inevitably fatal."

The cat's cradle is a clever device, totally used up as symbol. Anthropologists have noted that the game is almost universal among peoples of the world, linking the most aboriginal to the most sophisticated of modern cultures. As everybody knows, the game is played with a loop of string which, when transferred from the fingers of one player to those of another, assumes a different configuration. It is obviously different things to different people.

Like the duly famous Cheshire cat, this image fades until only the faintest suggestion is left. Hoenikker's dwarf-son, Newt, introduces it, citing the day of Hiroshima, when his father leered through the tangled web of a cat's cradle; that was the day his father smelled like the "mouth of Hell." For Hoenikker, a man who read nothing and was amused by the antics of matter in motion, a cat's cradle provided the sole means of diversion. Here, science is the chameleon figure, progressively less comprehensible to the laymen since the great innovators of the seventeenth century completed their investigations, infinite in its alterations, and ultimately destructive. The cradle next materializes in the domain of San Lorenzo's Albert Schweitzer analogue, Julian Castle. Newt paints a picture allegedly fraught with the enigmatic possibilities of Conrad's blindfolded lady in *Heart of Darkness*. Vonnegut's narrator leaps to the attack, only to be preempted by Newt, who, for all his lack of stature, manages to trample all doubts underfoot, murmuring coyly, "It's a Cat's Cradle." Now, art is the cat's cradle. But soon the tale of Angela's sad marital adventure materializes. Assuring the narrator of her woeful condition, Newt holds up his hands, stringless, but appropriately positioned: "See the cat? See the cradle?" And so, life is the cat's cradle. Finally, the conversation swings, as it sometimes must, to religion—and Newt simply says, without fanfare, "See the cat? See the cradle?"

To conclude the discourse on the obligations and failure of art, the narrator turns, muttering a line from Keats's "Ode on a Grecian Urn," remembering Angela's suicide by clarinet and Ice-Nine as he views the frozen Caribbean: art to artifact, the world remains, testifying to the failure of both God and man.

The good-humored broad-band eclecticism that marks Vonnegut's novels is in its most vigorous form in *Cat's Cradle*. A page opened at random discloses paraphrases of Dickens and Shakespeare, drawn through the writer's mind to the lines of the story by irresistible impulse. But there is consistency present in all discussions of "fix't fate" and free will. Free will cannot exist in the dead mechanical world of Vonnegut's perverse deity, who looks on unmoved as man moves through the unavoidable maze of his existence like a "piggywig" en route to slaughter, performing each act "as it was supposed to happen." The pseudo-religion and philosophy of Bokonon are unremarkable.

Science and war, of course, are the agents of malevolent destiny. Hoenikker's research for the marines produces Ice-Nine, and the predestined path of one plane of the San Lorenzan Air Force precipitates the final disaster. The twin offspring of technology and the idea of progress ride triumphant, for "science is the strongest thing there is." But, as a colleague of Hoenikker's ruefully remarks, "People [are] still superstitious instead of scientific."

Slaughterhouse-Five (published in 1969) is a blend of science fiction and the traditional novel, created in a variant of Vonnegut's random-intentional style. It is a story of time. In "Four Quartets," T. S. Eliot writes: "Time present and time past / Are perhaps both present in time future, / And time future contained in time past." So it is in Vonnegut's most successful novel, his most audacious effort at handling a novelist's most formidable bugaboo. In *Catch-22*, the piecemeal revelation of Snowden's death provides some sense of straight-line continuity; this gradual unfolding binds the book together. *Slaughterhouse-Five* is unified, however slightly, by the slender thread that is Billy Pilgrim's destined path. But he is "unstuck," sliding unpredictably along the axis of the fourth dimension. This is ironical. There are numerous other ironies, many based on themes and characters introduced in previous books. The result is occasionally tedious preciosity.

The authorial gimmick of discussing the difficulty of a feat while he performs it is not new to Vonnegut. Having feinted in this direction in *Mother Night* and *Cat's Cradle*, here he devotes the entire first chapter to the conception, history, and execution of *Slaughterhouse-Five*—by now a miracle of compression, according to the authorial voice of chapter 1. But as is always the case, author and narrator cannot be assumed identical. So the game begins. D. H. Lawrence's warning is always good advice: even the soberest and most objective of men, when he sets up to write of himself, exercises certain ineluctable editorial constraints and a deep bias, though perhaps unconscious that he does so. All of Vonnegut's prefatory explanation is in fact contained in chapter 1 of a work of fiction.

It is mildly surprising that an author whose thematic foundation has consistently involved war should be so concerned with writing an overtly identified antiwar book. Indeed, few who write of war intend to glorify it. Straightforward narrative is probably the best medium for placing war in its proper light. Thomas Boyd's depiction of World War I in *Through the Wheat* remains a classic example of that truth. But Vonnegut will write humorously of Dresden's death; the narrator is a new Democritus, as rendered by Robert Burton in *Anatomy of Melancholy*. When despair is too deep for tears, only laughter can prevail against it. Regrettably though, there is in *Slaughterhouse-Five* considerable evidence of the defect James Russell Lowell thought he saw in Burton's work, "A mire ankle-deep of deliberate confusion."

The twenty-odd shifts in time throughout *Slaughterhouse-Five* are confusing. The confusion stems not only from proliferated allusions, but from inconsistencies among the internal references in *Slaughterhouse-Five* and from some metamorphic alterations to persons and events summoned forth from earlier parts of the Vonnegut canon.

These phenomena are perhaps caused by a literary manifestation of the Fitzgerald deformation. Billy's birth occurred in 1922, but seldom does his announced age match the straightline arithmetic calculation. Billy is, according to the author, unstuck in time. He also moves freely in space. This is acceptable, though, as taught by Spengler, to whom space is a function of time. To the Tralfamadorians, as to Spengler and to Milton's God in *Paradise Lost*, time defines space, which then becomes a form of duration, thenceforward always present. Billy's expanding-radius, from amniotic sea to pangalactic space travel, marks the truly "involuntary and unqualified realization of depth" that "marks the frontier between child and . . . Man," according to Spengler.

The womb images so noticeable in Vonnegut appear now in clusters, like the ideas that delight the Tralfamadorians in their 4-D novels. Billy flashes back variously from prenatal warmth to a near-death which he found not unpleasant, in the bottom of the YMCA pool. His blanket in the hospital, the boxcar that almost becomes his tomb, the cool depths of the Carlsbad Caverns, and the bubble of Earth in the hostile cyanide of Tralfamadore—all are protective cubby-holes for Billy. On the rim of the Grand Canyon pre-teen Billy experiences fear. He is still light-years from the voyage to Tralfamadore. And it is the protective grotto under Schlachthof-Funf that "saves" Billy for his unavoidable rendezvous with Lazzaro's "lazer" gun in Chicago.

Vonnegut's prose attempts a robot-like equivalent to the potential T. S. Eliot expresses in the lines quoted earlier. Henri Bergson sees the relationship between time and space as the interaction of two media, one homogeneous (space) the other heterogeneous (time). In *Time and Free Will*, he speaks of duration as a continuous process in which the past "gnaws" through the present into the future, and, once occurring, is always present. "Pure duration," Bergson insists, occurs when the ego "lets itself live." These moments of pure duration are "internal and heterogeneous to one another." Because time is heterogeneous and infinitely protean, it will not yield to any approaches by "science." Further, these bits of ultimate human experience are unlike Stephen's Germanic version in the "Proteus" episode of *Ulysses*, neither "nacheinander" nor "nebeneinander." Not one-after-another, or one-beside-the-other, the moments of true duration in time are interpenetrating, like "notes from a tune" melting in the air, "elements which pass over into one another."

Billy's slipping and sliding through time sounds Bergsonian, but the image of "bugs in amber" is repeated throughout. Perhaps it is more appropriate to this technological context. It is more like Spengler: once generated in time, space remains, hardened, and—there. When Tralfamadorians look at stars they see spaghetti-like strands of light; when they look at man they see the protean being of the Sphinx's riddle. This is the long body of time. Once launched on his peregrinations, Billy soon learns part of his life by heart: all of it is always there.

Having interpreted the myth of Er in *God Bless You, Mr. Rosewater*, Vonnegut now addresses another central Platonic idea: the allegory of the cave. Whereas Plato's prisoner is constrained merely to look at pale secondary shadows of reality, the Tralfamadorian version of the human condition represents a victim cruelly fastened by steel to a rail-bound carriage. His head in a spherical device that allows no movement, the victim sees only a virtually dimensionless speck of light. He does see some of the actual, rather than shadows of imitation, but the safety of the cave is gone. Man hurtles through the infinite not even aware of motion. And the path is fixed.

Like Gulliver to the Houyhnhnms, Billy expounds on the unspeakable viciousness of his fellows on Earth. And just as he learns of war's literal universality, of the inevitable end, Billy is whisked back in time to the instant that he begets on vast Valencia a sterling Green Beret. The culpable space-exploring Tralfamadorian pilot always has and always will press the fatal starter button, igniting the Milky Way, "If it can be done, it must be done."

The characters from Vonnegut's past novels are flat here, with none of the rounded qualities the earlier books provided. But so it is when the "fundibulum" of one life randomly intersects those of others. Eliot still admires Kilgore Trout hugely, still despairs of his terrible prose. But here Eliot is merely an alcoholic former captain, quivering with guilt. Howard Campbell is the pure heavy, an American traitor recruiting for the Free America Corps. Bernard V. O'Hare is the narrator's boon companion, with none of the maniacal obsessions noted in *Mother Night*. Indeed, to read *Slaughterhouse-Five* without having read the preceding works is to perpetuate on an individual basis the sad state, metaphorically represented by "bugs in amber," that is the human lot in Vonnegut's universe. For it is true that all the other books illuminate *Slaughterhouse-Five*, even as it offers commentary back on them.

Player Piano documents the rise and fall of a revolution against technology in upstate New York. Technology's great moment o'erleaps the boundaries of space-time in the final, inter-galactic cataclysm, as the Tralfamadorians of *Slaughterhouse-Five* recount, unemotionally, the end of the Milky Way. The books in between tell of war between Earth and Mars, World War II (the chronological center of *Slaughterhouse-Five*), a minor revolt in the South American latitudes, and the end of the world, through Ice-Nine. The man who created Ice-Nine, as part of a research and development contract with the U.S. Marines, also presided over development of the bomb. But the end of Earth in *Cat's Cradle* still evokes Frost's "Fire and Ice," which points to the lowest circle of Dante's hell, the ice of the fraudulent. Cold, culpable Reason, with its hand maiden Progress lead to unexpected eschatological excitement. And it is fitting, too, that the end of the Milky Way should be the result of a slight Tralfamadorian oversight. Nothing personal, just something that happens—a predestined "accident."

In the entire sequence, only Eliot Rosewater is really human. He is irrational, concerned about people who fail. Temporarily "mad," he returns to reality just in time to hear the bird's helpful "Poo-tee-weet?" It is fully illuminating as T. S. Eliot's bird in another garden. Eliot is the only member of the Vonnegut universe to feel true guilt. It acts on him like a fortunate fall, precipitating the illness through which he must pass to regain his former health. Vonnegut's pessimism about human nature and free will is overwhelmingly evident throughout all his novels.

So it goes. The advent of irresistible progress brings with it the end of guilt, and the absolute extinction of hope. The same notes that provide the backdrop for Eliot's triumphant reversal of Mushari's plot against him conclude the action of *Slaughterhouse-Five*. But, going in circles, Billy Pilgrim moves always toward the cross-hairs of the waiting laser gun, on rails though "unstuck" in time. Perhaps it is the end of *Breakfast of Champions*, otherwise an undistinguished work, that resolves the chord awakened by the Eliots' earlier birds. Philboyd Studge offers the apple to his creation, Trout. For all the ranting about robots and bad juices attributable to a bumbling God who has since lost interest in His creation, the apple suggests Adam and the greater good precipitated by the advent of sin. If man loses his understanding of sin, there is no feeling of responsibility, and he becomes less than human. Like "Poo-tee-weet?" it cannot be reduced exactly to rational terms.

The works preceding *Breakfast of Champions* lie well within the parameters defining the "war novel" as examined in this study. In Vonnegut's universe there is no free will, and war is an inevitable by-product of the intercourse among nations. Given the human propensity for intraspecific killing, joined with the genie from reason's bottle—technological progress—the end is categorically predetermined, as in Milton's "De Doctrina Christiana." The possibility of choice exists, but mankind made it by following Galileo into the Faustian promised land. Vonnegut's work is a unique fusion of science fiction, secular despair, man's losing battle against technology, and a cyclical vision of the end, even for Indianapolis. And war provides the central theme for it all.

JAMES LUNDQUIST

The *"New Reality" of* Slaughterhouse-Five

"*It is my duty* to describe something beyond the imagination of mankind," the correspondent for the London *Times* began his dispatch in April 1945, after British troops marched into Belsen—the first Nazi prison camp to be exposed to world scrutiny—and discovered over forty thousand malnourished and dying prisoners and more than ten thousand corpses. The problem that Vonnegut faces in all of his novels is essentially the same as the one the correspondent had to face at Belsen—the increasing gap between the horrors of life in the twentieth century and our imaginative ability to comprehend their full actuality.

For Vonnegut, the subject matter is not simply Nazi atrocity; it is many other things—runaway technology, inflated views of human destiny, amoral science, the distribution of wealth in America, the senselessness of war as continued experience, and insanity in Midland City—but the aesthetic problem remains the same, whether the scene is the crystallization of the oceans or the firebombing of Dresden: How to conceptualize and define the night terrors of an era so unreal, so unbelievable, that the very term *fiction* seems no longer to have any currency.

Given the difficulty of the problem that dogs Vonnegut (and most contemporary novelists, for that matter), there is bound to be considerable debate concerning his success in solving it. The technique he employs in

From *Kurt Vonnegut*. © 1977 by Frederick Ungar Publishing Co., Inc.

Player Piano offers little in the way of innovation, and Vonnegut falls considerably short of making a computerized future seem all that frightening. There are troublesome deficiencies in some of his other novels as well—the science-fiction motifs in *The Sirens of Titan*, as humorously as they are used, occasionally seem hackneyed; the flat characterization in *God Bless You, Mr. Rosewater* makes it difficult to see Eliot Rosewater as much more than a "tinhorn saint"; and Vonnegut's own appearance at the Holiday Inn cocktail lounge near the end of *Breakfast of Champions* is, just about any way one looks at it, a little contrived.

These are, of course, not major objections to any of the novels cited, and good arguments could be made for their artistic merit on other grounds. But there have been sustained attacks on Vonnegut's writing ever since the start of his career, doubts that were pretty well summed up in P. S. Prescott's strident review of *Breakfast of Champions*. "From time to time, it's nice to have a book you can hate—it clears the pipes—and I hate this book for its preciousness, its condescension to its characters, its self-indulgence, and its facile fatalism: all the lonely people, their fates sealed in epoxy," Prescott writes. "Mostly I hate it for its reductiveness, its labored denial of man's complexity and resilience. Life cannot, as Vonnegut insists, be summed up with 'and so on' and 'ETC.'—or at least not without more wit and insight than Vonnegut can master."

Such attacks are not a symptom of vindictiveness alone. To many critics, Vonnegut's novels do read as if they are haphazard in structure and simplistic in thought. Robert Scholes has tried to reply to all this by pointing out that "Serious critics have shown some reluctance to acknowledge that Vonnegut is among the great writers of his generation. He is . . . both too funny and too intelligent for many, who confuse muddled earnestness with profundity." But the only effective reply is to take a close look at what is probably Vonnegut's most widely read novel and perhaps his best, *Slaughterhouse-Five*.

"I felt after I finished *Slaughterhouse-Five* that I didn't have to write at all anymore if I didn't want to," Vonnegut has said. "It was the end of some sort of career." *Slaughterhouse-Five*, with its non-linear time scheme and its complex interweaving of science-fiction fantasy and the realities of World War II, makes his earlier novels, as innovative as some of them are, appear to be ordinary and uncomplicated by comparison, even if they are far from being that. The reason for this is that Vonnegut reveals himself in *Slaughterhouse-Five*, as do Alexander Trocchi in *Cain's Book* and Thomas Pynchon in *V*, to be "highly self-conscious of the novel as an abstract concept that examines a condition that never yields itself up completely as itself." In other words, the novel functions to reveal new viewpoints in somewhat the same way that the theory of relativity broke through the concepts of absolute space and time. *Slaughterhouse-Five* thus gains its structure from Vonnegut's essential aesthetic problem—how to describe a reality that is beyond human imagination.

The method he chooses is outlined in the explanation given Billy Pilgrim of the Tralfamadorian novel as he is being transported toward that whimsical planet. His captors offer him the only book in English they have, Jacqueline Susann's *Valley of the Dolls*, which is to be placed in a museum. "Billy read it, thought it was pretty good in spots," Vonnegut writes. "The people in it certainly had their ups and downs. But Billy didn't want to read about the same ups and downs over and over again."

The Tralfamadorians allow him to look at some of their novels, but warn that he cannot begin to understand them. The books are small; it would take a dozen of them to even approach *Valley of the Dolls* in bulk, and the language is impossible for Billy. But he can see that the novels consist of clumps of symbols with stars in between. Billy is told that the clumps function something like telegrams, with each clump a message about a situation or scene. But the clumps are not read sequentially as the chapters are in an earthling novel of the ordinary sort. They are read simultaneously. "There isn't any particular relationship between all the messages," the speaker says to Billy, "except that the author has chosen them carefully, so that, when seen all at once, they produce an image of life that is beautiful and surprising and deep. There is no beginning, no middle, no end, no suspense, no moral, no causes, no effects. What we love in our books are the depths of many marvelous moments seen all at one time."

Slaughterhouse-Five is an approximation of this type of novel. Its chapters are divided into short sections (clumps if you will), seldom more than a few paragraphs long. The time-tripping, both by Billy and the narrator, produces an effect somewhat like that achieved in the Tralfamadorian novel—to see many moments at once. The time-tripping also serves to eliminate suspense. (We know not only of Billy's assassination long before the novel ends, but also how the universe will end—the Tralfamadorians blow it up experimenting with a new fuel for their flying saucers.) And the conclusion Vonnegut comes to after examining the causes and effects of Dresden is that there indeed is no moral, only the *Poo-tee-weet* of the bird call that Billy hears when he discovers that the war in Europe is over and he wanders out onto the shady streets of springtime Dresden.

What the Tralfamadorian structure does for Vonnegut is to enable him to embody a new reality in his novel—at least new in contrast to the sequential ups-and-downs reality of the traditional novel. Vonnegut's method accords well with the major changes in the conception of physical reality that have come out of contemporary science. "Change, ambiguity, and subjectivity (in a sense these are synonyms) thus become ways of defining human reality," Jerry H. Bryant writes in commenting on the relationship between twentieth-century physics and recent fiction. "Novelist after novelist examines these features, and expresses almost universal frustration at being deprived of the old stability of metaphysical reality." But not Vonnegut. His Tralfamadorian scheme enables him to overcome the problems of change, ambiguity, and subjectivity involved in objectifying the events surrounding the fire-bombing of Dresden and the involvement of Billy Pilgrim and the author in them.

This is a difficult idea, but one way to understand it is to consider the distinction Bertrand Russell makes in *The ABC of Relativity* between the old view of matter (that it has a definite identity in space and time) and the new view (that it is an event). "An event does not persist and move, like the traditional piece of matter," Russell writes; "it merely exists for a little moment then ceases. A piece of matter will thus be resolved into a series of events. . . . The whole series of these events makes up the whole history of the particle, and the particle is regarded as *being* its history, not some metaphysical entity to which things happen."

This is just the paradoxical conception of Billy that Vonnegut develops. Billy at first seems to be merely an entity to which things happen—he is lost behind the lines during the Battle of the Bulge, he and Roland Weary are captured by the Germans, he survives the fire-bombing of Dresden, he marries, he is the sole survivor of a plane crash, he hallucinates that he is kidnapped by the Tralfamadorians, he appears on crackpot talk-shows, and he is finally gunned down in Chicago. But through the constant movement back and forth in time that constitutes Vonnegut's narrative, we see Billy becoming his history, existing all at once, as if he is an electron. And this gives the novel a structure that is, to directly state the analogy, atomic. Billy whirls around the central fact of Dresden, the planes of his orbits constantly intersecting, and where he has been, he will be.

Of course, all of Vonnegut's earlier central characters are somewhat like Billy in that they are seen as aspects of a protean reality. (Again, the name of Paul Proteus suggests how persistent this representation of personality is.) But it is not until *Slaughterhouse-Five* that Vonnegut develops a way of fully representing the context of that reality. The sudden changes that come over Malachi Constant, Eliot Rosewater, and others make them seem as illusive and problematic as the absurd universe they occupy. By oversimplifying his characters, Vonnegut does manage to suggest something of the complexity of human nature by indirection. But they still tend to linger in the mind as cartoon figures (the Dell paperback covers of *The Sirens of Titan* and *Mother Night* certainly suggest so).

This is not the case with Billy Pilgrim. The Tralfamadorian structure through which his story is told (*sent* might be a better word) gives Billy dimension and substance and brings him eerily to life despite his pale ineffectuality. "Vonnegut's reluctance to depict well-developed characters and to supply them with conventional motives for their actions serves as a conscious burlesque of the whole concept of realism in the novel," Charles B. Harris in his study of the contemporary novel of the absurd has pointed out. But with *Slaughterhouse-Five*, the conscious burlesque is diminished because Vonnegut has come up with a representation of Billy Pilgrim's universe that is in itself a new concept of realism—or reality.

Slaughterhouse-Five is thus as much a novel about writing novels as it is an account of Billy Pilgrim and Dresden. In relating the difficulty he had in dealing with Dresden, Vonnegut prefaces *Slaughterhouse-Five* with an account of his own pilgrimages through time as he tried to write about his Dresden experience. The opening section consists of jumps back and forth in the author's life—from his return to Dresden on a Guggenheim grant to his return home from the war two decades earlier, from a conversation on the telephone with his old war buddy to the end of the war in a beet field on the Elbe outside of Halle, and then on to the Chicago City News Bureau, Schenectady and General Electric, visiting O'Hare in Pennsylvania, teaching writing at the University of Iowa, and then Dresden and the Guggenheim trip once more.

The concern is always with the problem of writing the book—how to represent imaginatively things that are unimaginable—but in detailing his frustrations, Vonnegut conceptualizes his own life the way he later does Billy's, in terms of Tralfamadorian time theory. The structure of the chapter about writing the novel consequently prefigures the structure of the novel itself.

In that opening section, Vonnegut outlines his essential difficulty by elaborating on the misconception with which he began work on the novel. He states that he thought the book would be easy to write—all he would have to do is to simply report what he had seen. But this does not work. Too many other things get in the way. Why was Dresden, a supposedly safe city, bombed? Why did the American and British governments cover up the facts about the raid? What does the Dresden attack imply about American and British civilization? And, more important, why must Vonnegut's life always lead up to and go back to what he saw when he emerged from the slaughterhouse meat locker and looked at the moonscape that was once perhaps the most beautiful city in Europe?

The conflict Vonnegut is indicating is that of the old Henry James–H. G. Wells debate on what the novel as a literary form should be. James felt that it should be mimetic, realistic, that it should relate human experience as accurately as possible through detailed characterization and careful construction. Wells, on the other hand, believed that social pronouncements and ideas are more important, and that art should be subordinate to both. Wells was not even certain that the novel should be taken seriously as an art form. For him, characterization was just something to be got through so that an idea or a "ventilation" of the novel's social, political, or philosophical point can be got across as clearly as possible.

Wells's influence is certainly a factor in the development of the science-fiction novel, and James must be taken into account in any discussion of the so-called mainstream or art novel. Vonnegut, as he indicates in his preface to *Slaughterhouse-Five*, is caught somewhere in the middle of the debate. His earlier books are mainly novels of character written to a thesis, an approach that leads to the direct statement of a moral in *Mother Night*.

But *Slaughterhouse-Five* is different; Vonnegut's impulse is to begin with his own experience, not with characters or ideas, but the ideas soon get in the way.

Two structural possibilities come to mind. The first is suggested in the song Vonnegut remembers as he thinks about how useless, yet how obsessive, the Dresden part of his memory has been:

> My name is Yon Yonson,
> I work in Wisconsin,
> I work in a lumbermill there,
> The people I meet when I walk down the street,
> They say, "What's your name?"
> And I say,
> "My name is Yon Yonson,
> I work in Wisconsin. . . ."

When people ask him what *he* is working on, Vonnegut says that for years he has been telling them the same thing—a book about Dresden. Like Yon Yonson, he seems doomed to repeat the answer endlessly. But the maddening song suggests something else—the tendency many people (perhaps all) have to return to a central point in their lives in reply to the question of identity ("What's your name?").

The song also crudely suggests the time theory that is later developed in the novel with its emphasis on infinite repetition. But repetition leads nowhere, especially in a novel, so Vonnegut considers another possibility. He takes a roll of wallpaper, and on the back of it tries to make an outline of the story using his daughter's crayons (a different color for each of the characters). "And the blue line met the red line and then the yellow line,"

Vonnegut writes, "and the yellow line stopped because the character represented by the yellow line was dead. And so on. The destruction of Dresden was represented by a vertical band of orange cross-hatching, and all the lines that were still alive passed through it, came out the other side." This is an outline for a Jamesian novel with an essentially linear time scheme. But it does not work as a representation of the experience Vonnegut is anxious to write about.

For one thing, characters do not actually come out the other side and inevitably go on from there. Like Vonnegut himself, like Yon Yonson, they compulsively return, moving back and forth on their lines. And as for the lines that stop, the beginning and middle of those lines are still there. What does Vonnegut do? He comes up with a structure that includes both the Yon Yonson story and the wallpaper outline. It is as if he rolls the wallpaper into a tube so all of the characters and incidents are closely layered, so they are in effect one unit, and the reader must look at them from the side. The tube then becomes a telescope through which the reader looks into the fourth dimension, or at least into another dimension of the novel. The story goes around and around, yet it still leads somewhere, and yet the end is very close to the beginning.

It may well be that, as Karen and Charles Wood suggest, *Slaughterhouse-Five* is a new form of novel repesenting the mature fusion of science fiction and Jamesian literature of experience.

The search for an approach also takes Vonnegut through an investigation of other works of literature that deal with catastrophe and the attitudes that surround it. He mentions an account of the Children's Crusade in a nineteenth-century book, *Extraordinary Popular Delusions and the Madness of Crowds*. This account is used to underscore the contrast he draws between the serious business of war and the naiveté of Billy Pilgrim, Roland Weary, and most of the other soldiers he depicts. He mentions *Dresden, History, Stage and Gallery*, by Mary Endell (published 1908), and its account of how Dresden, with all of its beauty, has been attacked repeatedly.

He quotes some lines from Theodore Roethke's *Words for the Wind* to suggest both his own confusion and the sense he has that, simply by moving ahead and back in time, the meaning of Dresden was being sorted out:

I wake to sleep, and take my waking slow.
I feel my fate in what I cannot fear.
I learn by going where I have to go.

He mentions Erica Ostrovsky's *Céline and His Vision* and recounts how death and time also obsessed the insomniac French writer after he was wounded in World War I. And then he mentions the story of the destruction of Sodom and Gomorrah in the Bible and how Lot's wife, because of her compulsive looking back at the burning cities when she was told not to, was turned into a pillar of salt.

All of these references either give Vonnegut ideas and material or else they relate to his own reaction to Dresden, but they do not quite offer him the approach he is after. This, as we have seen, he had to discover for himself.

The structure Vonnegut chooses is indicated right at the start of Billy Pilgrim's story. It is a structure that, for all of the later explanation and illustration of its basis in Tralfamadorian time theory, actually develops out of Vonnegut's central character. Vonnegut, in the guise of an oral storyteller, asks us to "Listen." Then, in two paragraphs he introduces Billy and sets up the pattern that will be followed throughout the rest of the novel: "Billy Pilgrim has come unstuck in time. . . . He has seen his birth and death many times, he says, and pays random visits to all the events in between."

Vonnegut proceeds to outline Billy's life in the next few pages—what happens to him during the war, his marriage, the airplane crash, the flying saucer, and his appearances on talk shows—to build irony and to bring out the sudden and often absurdly sad changes in Billy's life that make his time-tripping largely a survival reaction.

Billy's survival seems at first to depend simply on his thinness as a character, his ineffectuality, and his utter insignificance. But the imagery associated with Billy, as it expands and cuts back and forth through the novel, suggests otherwise. He is said at times to look like a Coke bottle in shape and like a filthy flamingo in dress, and he is said to have a "chest and shoulders like a box of kitchen matches." But before his capture by the Germans he is portrayed "like a poet in the Parthenon." When he is elected president of the Ilium Lions Club in 1957, he gets up to give his acceptance speech in a voice that is a "gorgeous instrument." He becomes as "rich as Croesus." At another point in his travels through time, he is clearly identified with Christ, "self-crucified, holding himself there with a blue and ivory claw hooked over the sill of the ventilator." Billy is anything but a thin character; he is another illustration of Vonnegut's concept of Protean man. Billy *needs* to travel back and forth in time not only to understand himself but also to endure himself, to become his history. He is many personalities, many selves existing together at once. He is a living Tralfamadorian "clump."

One of the surprises in the novel is that the personality that seems the most ridiculous—Billy as an optometrist—turns out to be the most important symbolically. Throughout the novel there is considerable emphasis on seeing things, and there is a near continuous contrast between the way the world looks to Billy and the way others see him. At times Billy appears to be a poet and at other times, such as when he appears in Dresden wrapped in an azure curtain and wearing silver-painted combat boots, he looks the fool. For Billy himself, there is considerable development in the way he views what has happened to him.

The change that comes over Billy is mainly a result of the way he is forced to look at many things—Weary's triangular-bladed knife with its brass-knuckle grip, the picture of a woman attempting sexual intercourse with a Shetland pony, the German corporal's boots (in which Billy sees a vision of Adam and Eve), his Cadillac El Dorado Coupe de Ville in the suburban shopping center parking lot outside his office, the spastic salesman who comes to the door trying to peddle phony magazine subscriptions, St. Elmo's fire around the heads of the guards and his fellow prisoners, the cozy interior of the guards' railroad car, the clock on his gas stove an hour before the flying saucer comes to pick him up, the backward movie he watches on television while he is waiting for the Tralfamadorians, and so on. Through recapitulating imagery, Vonnegut suggests how the simultaneous relationship of everything Billy sees and experiences is slowly revealed and how Tralfamadorian time theory, instead of merely being a comic example of Vonnegut's fondness for science-fiction motifs, develops naturally and logically out of Billy's unconscious awareness of his own life.

Vonnegut's use of recapitulating imagery can be seen on almost every page of the novel, but the backward movie will serve as one of the best examples of this technique. Billy suddenly sees a movie of World War II running backward in his head. The bombers suck the fire and the bombs back into their bellies, the bombs are shipped back to the factories and dismantled, and the dangerous contents are reduced to mineral form and returned to the ground. The fliers turn in their uniforms and become high-school kids. Hitler and everyone else turns into a baby and, as Vonnegut writes, "all humanity, without exception, conspired biologically to produce two perfect people named Adam and Eve. . . ." The reference to Adam and Eve recapitulates the vision Billy saw in the German corporal's boot years before; and the barking of the dog he hears outside his house recapitulates the barking Billy heard just before the corporal captured him.

A further use of this type of imagery occurs when Billy hears what he thinks is the cry of a melodious owl, but the sound turns out to be the whine of the flying saucer. All his professional life he has been working with an "owl" of another sort. During one of his time trips, Billy opens his eyes and finds himself "staring into the glass eyes of a jade green mechanical owl. The owl was hanging upside down from a rod of stainless steel. The owl was Billy's optometer in his office in Ilium. An optometer is an instrument for measuring refractive errors in eyes—in order that corrective lenses may be prescribed." With this recapitulation of imagery, a major theme in the novel is brought into focus.

Of all that Billy is forced to look at, the most significant is what is revealed to him by the Tralfamadorians. The flying saucer becomes an optometer that measures the refractive errors in Billy's outlook and the Tralfamadorians are able to suggest a prescription. But it is Billy's job as an optometrist to help others see, and this is what he tries to do. At first, he is not very effective. He is able to attend the Ilium School of Optometry for only one semester before he is drafted (and he is enrolled only in *night* sessions at that). And after the war, despite all his success, Billy is dealing less in vision than in fashion: "Frames are where the money is." But through his flying-saucer journey, he gains a new conception of what his job should be— prescribing "corrective lenses for Earthling souls" so that they can see into the fourth dimension as the Tralfamadorians do.

This development of Billy's vision is handled in a deceptively ambiguous way, of course. The repetition of imagery together with the juxtaposition of disparate events in Billy's life suggests that his trip to Tralfamadore is an hallucination and that the prescription he winds up advocating is essentially the result of the associative powers of his mind. The substance of his trip to Tralfamadore may well be the consequence of reading a Kilgore Trout novel, and the whole business of time travel and the simultaneous existence of events may well be simply another of the human illusions Vonnegut attacks so frequently in his earlier novels.

But the point for Billy is that the Tralfamadorians *are* real, that the years of his life are the only time there is, and he is going to live every moment over and over again. In addition, there is the pragmatic value of his vision—it enables him to deal with the horror of Dresden and to get around the question of "Why me?" that echoes through the novel. Are his lenses rose-colored or not? It perhaps depends on the reader's own willingness to look into the fourth dimension with him. *Slaughterhouse-Five*, at any rate, gives us a glimpse of what that dimension might be like, and shows us at the very least how it is possible to gain a sense of purpose in life by doing what Billy Pilgrim does—he re-invents himself and his universe.

The process of re-invention is made vivid by Vonnegut's style with its hesitant short sentences and his tendency to return again and again to the same images. His abruptness works well in describing the time shifts Billy suddenly goes through, and it contributes a sense of Billy's new vision, his re-invented universe, being formulated piece by piece. But the overall effect of the direct, often choppy, sentences and the brief paragraphs (several times consisting of only a few words) is to suggest the whirring of basic particles, of electrons that really cannot be seen. What we think of when we think of the structure of the atom is not actually there at all—it is only a model, an illusion. And the same thing can be said of *Slaughterhouse-Five* and Billy Pilgrim's erratic revolutions in time around Dresden. But as a model, it is, through its recapitulating imagery, its optometric symbolism, its positively charged sentences, and its telegraphic-Tralfamadorian-atomic structure, one of the best solutions we have to the problem of describing the unimaginable.

Unfortunately, one cannot say the same of the movie version of the novel released in 1972. Although Michael Sacks as Billy Pilgrim and Valerie Perrine as Montana Wildhack are effective and director George Roy Hill (who also directed *Butch Cassidy and the Sundance Kid*) and writer Stephen Geller treat the story with reverence, the film does not match the sophistication of statement to be found in the book. One problem is that while Billy's time-tripping is handled in an artistically justifying way by Vonnegut, it is merely cinematically familiar on the screen where flashbacks and flash-forwards only serve to diminish its intellectual force.

There are many nice touches in the film, however. One is Billy's changing into Nazi-looking steel-rimmed glasses in middle age (a device that hints at the recapitulating imagery in the novel). And there are some brilliantly conceived scenes, such as one of American soldiers marching through Dresden, past the spires and statues of the city, while the Fourth Brandenburg Concerto comes over the soundtrack. Much of the film was shot in Prague by Miroslav Ondricek, the Czech photographer who did Forman's *Loves of a Blonde* and Ivan Passer's *Intimate Lightning*, and Ondricek deserves much of the credit for the visually pleasing aspects of the production. But, as one reviewer wrote, "In its elaborate structure and editing, its leaping bounds between fact and fancy, the film is like a version of *Last Year in Marienbad* revised for showing on *Sesame Street*."

Of course, no film could document the way Vonnegut confronted his own ambiguous nature in working out the story of Billy Pilgrim. The character who is developed the most fully in the novel is Vonnegut himself. This is why Vonnegut can get away with repeating the phrase, "So it goes," after every tragic or pathetic incident. He has established himself, through his preface, as one of the characters in the book. His is a human voice, not just that of an omniscient narrator, and this in itself adds poignancy to the inhuman acts his subject matter forces him to describe.

Vonnegut's way of dealing with that subject matter results in a novel that is, by any standard, highly complex. It is a novel that works toward the resolution of Vonnegut's own obsessions at the same time it works toward the resolution of several nervous questions concerning the viability of the genre itself. Like many of his contemporaries, Vonnegut accepts the idea of an absurd universe that is chaotic and without meaning. But unlike Beckett and

Robbe-Grillet, he does not develop an anti-style, even though he seems to share their fear of the loss of distinctions between fact and fiction. Instead, he chooses to rely upon many traditional devices (among them burlesque and parody) in conjunction with the new reality of twentieth-century physics and the motifs of science fiction to come up with a radical use of fictional form that reveals a regained joy in storytelling and is also true to his cosmically ironic vision.

ROBERT MERRILL AND PETER A. SCHOLL

Vonnegut's Slaughterhouse-Five: *The Requirements of Chaos*

> I like Utopian talk, speculation about what
> our planet should be, anger about what our
> planet is.
>
> —Kurt Vonnegut, Jr.

In a recent issue of *SAF*, Lynn Buck presents a view of Kurt Vonnegut which has become depressingly popular. Her very title, "Vonnegut's World of Comic Futility," suggests the drift of her discussion. Professor Buck speaks of Vonnegut's "deliberate mechanization of mankind," "the cynicism of the comical world he has created," and his "nihilistic message." She concludes at one point that "to enter Vonnegut's world, one must abide by his rules, unencumbered by man-centered notions about the universe." There is some question, however, as to whether Buck is a reliable guide concerning the nature of these "rules." Her Vonnegut is a man who cautions against "man-centered notions about the universe," whereas the real Kurt Vonnegut once told a group of Bennington graduates, "Military science is probably right about the contemptibility of man in the vastness of the universe. Still—I deny that contemptibility, and I beg you to deny it." Her Vonnegut is cynical and nihilistic, whereas the real Kurt Vonnegut recently said, "My longer-range schemes have to do with providing all Americans with artificial extended families of a thousand members or more. Only when we have overcome

From *Studies in American Fiction* 6, no. 1 (Spring 1978). © 1978 by Northeastern University.

loneliness can we begin to share wealth and work more fairly. I honestly believe that we will have those families by-and-by, and I hope they will become international." In short, Buck's Vonnegut is a fiction. Vonnegut's readers know that he himself believes in certain kinds of fictions, "harmless untruths" which he calls *foma*. But Buck's version of Vonnegut is not harmless, for it leads her to distort the meaning of everything Vonnegut has written.

This reading of Vonnegut is all too representative. Repeatedly Vonnegut's critics have argued that his novels embody the cynical essence of Black Humor, a form so despairing as to contrast even with the relatively dark novels of a writer like Hemingway. The result has been a thorough misunderstanding of Vonnegut's vision in general and the meaning of his novels in particular. The distortion is most serious with Vonnegut's sixth novel, *Slaughterhouse-Five* (1969), for this is his one book that has a real claim to be taken seriously as a first-rate work of art. For this reason, it is crucial that the novel be interpreted properly. To do this, the notion that Vonnegut's world is one of comic futility must be abandoned. It must be seen that Vonnegut's advice to the Bennington graduates is embodied in his novels as well.

> But I continue to believe that artists—all artists—should be
> treasured as alarm systems.
>
> Kurt Vonnegut, Jr.

It is safe to assume that novels of social protest are not written by cynics or nihilists. Surely protest implies the belief that man's faults are remediable. It is relevant, then, that Vonnegut's novels, early and late, were conceived in the spirit of social protest. Vonnegut has said that his motives as a writer are "political": "I agree with Stalin and Hitler and Mussolini that the writer should serve his society. I differ with dictators as to *how* writers should serve. Mainly, I think they should be—and biologically *have* to be—agents of change." This belief informs Vonnegut's first book, *Player Piano* (1952), a novel which deserves Leslie Fiedler's elegant complaint that it is excessively committed to "proving (once more?) that machines deball and dehumanize men." It is crucial to *Mother Night* (1961), a novel which has a rather unquietistic "moral" if the author's 1966 introduction is to be believed: "We are what we pretend to be, so we must be careful about what we pretend to be." And it is no less central to *God Bless You, Mr. Rosewater* (1965), a novel in which Vonnegut's attack on capitalistic practices is unrelenting. These books were all written by the man who once said that he admired George Orwell "almost more than any other man." They were written by the man who likes Utopian talk, speculation about what Earth should be, anger about what the planet is.

Therefore, it is hard to believe that *Slaughterhouse-Five* is a novel that recommends "resigned acceptance" as the proper response to life's injustices.

Tony Tanner is the only critic who has used the term "quietism" in discussing *Slaughterhouse-Five*, but most of Vonnegut's critics seem intent on reading the book as if it *were* the work of a quietist. The problem concerns Vonnegut's "hero," Billy Pilgrim. *Slaughterhouse-Five* is about Pilgrim's response to the fire-bombing of Dresden. This response includes Billy's supposed space-travel to the planet Tralfamadore, where he makes the rather startling discovery about time that Winston Miles Rumfoord first made in Vonnegut's second novel, *The Sirens of Titan* (1959), "that everything that ever has been always will be, and everything that ever will be always has been." This proves immensely satisfying to Pilgrim, for it means "that when a person dies he only *appears* to die. He is still very much alive in the past, so it is very silly for people to cry at his funeral." Indeed, it is very silly for people to cry about anything, including Dresden. This is the "wisdom" Billy achieves in the course of Vonnegut's novel. It is, of course, the wisdom of quietism. If everything that ever has been always will be, and everything that ever will be always has been, nothing can be done to change the drift of human affairs. As the Tralfamadorians tell Billy Pilgrim, the notion of free will is a quaint Earthling illusion.

What is more disturbing, Vonnegut's critics seem to think that he is saying the same thing. For Anthony Burgess, "*Slaughterhouse* is a kind of evasion—in a sense like J. M. Barrie's *Peter Pan*—in which we're being told to carry the horror of the Dresden bombing and everything it implies up to a level of fantasy. . . ." For Charles Harris, "The main idea emerging from *Slaughterhouse-Five* seems to be that the proper response to life is one of resigned acceptance." For Alfred Kazin, "Vonnegut deprecates any attempt to see tragedy that day in Dresden. . . . He likes to say with arch fatalism, citing one horror after another, 'So it goes.'" For Tanner, "Vonnegut has . . . total sympathy with such quietistic impulses." And the same notion is found throughout *The Vonnegut Statement*, a book of original essays written and collected by Vonnegut's most loyal academic "fans."

This view of Vonnegut's book tends to contradict what he has said in published interviews and his earlier novels. But of course the work itself must be examined to determine whether or not *Slaughterhouse-Five* is a protest novel. Such a study should reveal Vonnegut's complex strategy for protesting such horrors as Dresden.

> If all time is eternally present
> All time is unredeemable.
>
> "Burnt Norton"
>
> When you're dead you're dead.
>
> Kurt Vonnegut, Jr.

The key to Vonnegut's strategy is his striking introduction of the Tralfamadorians into what he calls an antiwar novel. The fire-bombing of Dresden actually receives less emphasis than Billy Pilgrim's space and time travel, especially his visit with the Tralfamadorians. Vonnegut has played down the immediate impact of the war in order to make "a powerful little statement about the kinds of social attitudes responsible for war and its atrocities," as Harris has remarked of *Mother Night*. By transporting his hero to Tralfamadore, Vonnegut is able to introduce the Tralfamadorian notions about time and death which inevitably call attention to more "human" theories. The status of the Tralfamadorians is therefore the most important issue in any discussion of *Slaughterhouse-Five*.

It is the status of the Tralfamadorians themselves which is in question, not just their ideas. Vonnegut offers many hints that the Tralfamadorians do not exist. Just before he goes on a radio talk show to spread the Tralfamadorian gospel, Billy Pilgrim comes across several books by Kilgore Trout in a Forty-second Street porno shop:

> The titles were all new to him, or he thought they were. Now he opened one. . . . The name of the book was *The Big Board*. He got a few paragraphs into it, and then realized that he *had* read it before—years ago, in the veterans' hospital. It was about an Earthling man and woman who were kidnapped by extraterrestrials. They were put on display on a planet called Zircon-212.

It seems that the scenario of Billy's life in outer space is something less than original. Pilgrim gets his "idea" for Tralfamadore from Kilgore Trout, just as Dwayne Hoover gets his ideas from Trout in *Breakfast of Champions* (1973). Perhaps this is what Vonnegut had in mind when he said that "*Slaughterhouse* and *Breakfast* used to be one book." The parallel is instructive, for Hoover is clearly insane. Pilgrim may not literally be insane, but Vonnegut has undermined the reality of his experience on Tralfamadore. Indeed, the conclusion is irresistible that Pilgrim's space and time travel are modes of escape. Surely it is not coincidental that Billy first time-travels just as he is about to lie down and die during the Battle of the Bulge, nor that he begins to speak of his trip to Tralfamadore *after* his airplane crash in 1968. Faced with the sheer horror of life, epitomized by World War II and especially the fire-bombing of Dresden, Billy "escapes" to Tralfamadore.

If the very existence of Tralfamadore is in doubt, one might wonder about the ideas Billy Pilgrim encounters there. Billy takes great comfort in these ideas, but at first glance there would seem to be nothing very heartening in the Tralfamadorian philosophy. After all, the Tralfamadorians think of human beings as "bugs in amber." Like bugs, human beings are trapped in *structured* moments that have always existed and always will exist. For that matter, human beings are not really human: "Tralfamadorians, of course, say that every creature and plant in the universe is a machine." The Tralfamadorians would seem to be as jovial about life as the later Mark Twain.

But the Tralfamadorians have much to offer in the way of consolation. Most crucially, their theory of time denies the reality of death. Further, it allows man to pick and choose among the eternal moments of his existence. If everything that ever has been always will be, one can practice the Tralfamadorian creed and "ignore the awful times, and concentrate on the good ones." If one concentrates hard enough, he can have the same epitaph as Billy Pilgrim: "Everything was beautiful and nothing hurt." He can be like Billy in other ways, too. He can survive such demoralizing experiences as Dresden. He can return home and complete his education, marry the boss's daughter, make $60,000 a year, father a daughter as capable as Barbara Pilgrim and a son who finally gets "straightened out" by the Green Berets; he can own a fifth of the new Holiday Inn in town and half of three Tastee-Freeze stands; he can be President of the Lions Club and drive Cadillacs with such stickers as "Impeach Earl Warren" and "Reagan for President." He can not only get by, he can thrive.

But all this can be done only by ignoring the wisdom embodied in Billy Pilgrim's prayer: "God grant me the serenity to accept the things I cannot change, courage to change the things I can, and wisdom always to tell the difference." This advice is meaningless for Billy himself, for "among the things Billy Pilgrim could not change were the past, the present, and the future." Billy is one of those people Vonnegut was referring to when he said "there are people, particularly dumb people, who are in terrible trouble and never get out of it, because they're not intelligent enough. And it strikes me as gruesome and comical that in our culture we have an expectation that a man can always solve his problems." Billy is a man who can only solve his problems by saying that they are insoluble.

The irony here is that the Billy Pilgrims of this world *are* better off saying that everything is beautiful and nothing hurts, for they truly cannot change the past, the present, or the future. All they can do is survive. Tralfamadore is a fantasy, a desperate attempt to rationalize chaos, but one must sympathize with Billy's need to create Tralfamadore. After all, the need for supreme fictions is a very human trait. As one of Vonnegut's characters tells a psychiatrist, "I think you guys are going to have to come up with a lot of wonderful new lies, or people just aren't going to want to go on living."

The need for such "lies" is almost universal in *Slaughterhouse-Five*. Most obviously, it lies behind Roland Weary's pathetic dramatization of himself and two companions as The Three Musketeers. It is most poignantly suggested in the religiosity of Billy's mother, who develops "a terrible hankering for a crucifix" even though she never joins a church and in fact has no real faith. Billy's mother finally does buy a crucifix from a Sante Fe gift shop, and Vonnegut's comment is crucial to much else in the book: "Like so many Americans, she was trying to construct a life that made sense from things she found in gift shops." Billy Pilgrim's "lie" is no less human and a good deal more "wonderful."

But finally Billy Pilgrim is not Everyman. One may sympathize with his attempt to make sense of things, but the fact remains that some men have greater resources than others. Indeed, some men are like Kurt Vonnegut. By intruding into his own tale, Vonnegut contrasts his personal position with that of his protagonist. Billy Pilgrim preaches the Tralfamadorian theory of time until he becomes a latter-day Billy Graham; Vonnegut looks with anguish at a clock he wants to go faster and remarks, "There was nothing I could do about it. As an Earthling, I had to believe whatever clocks said—and calendars." Billy Pilgrim sends his sons to Vietnam and the Green Berets; Vonnegut tells his sons "that they are not under any circumstances to take part in massacres, and that the news of massacres of enemies is not to fill them with satisfaction or glee." Vonnegut even tells his sons "not to work for companies which make massacre machinery, and to express contempt for people who think we need machinery like that." Billy Pilgrim says that God was right when He commanded Lot's wife not to look back upon Sodom and Gomorrah; Vonnegut writes *Slaughterhouse-Five* and so becomes "a pillar of salt" himself. As Donald Greiner has said, "while Billy can come to terms with death and Dresden, Vonnegut cannot." Nor can anyone who would be fully human.

This should be clear from a careful reading of Vonnegut's first chapter. Vonnegut's discussion of how he wrote *Slaughterhouse-Five* is not an indulgence, for his difficulties in writing the book are as crucial to its meaning as the story of Billy Pilgrim. As a "trafficker in climaxes and thrills and characterizations and wonderful dialogue and suspense and confrontations," Vonnegut is supposed to create fictions with beginnings, middles, and ends. But how does one create such a structure from the materials of Dresden? One can follow Billy Pilgrim to Tralfamadore and write the Tralfamadorian equivalent of the novel, books which appear to be "brief clumps of symbols separated by stars," where each clump of symbols is "a brief, urgent message" and "there is no beginning, no middle, no end, no suspense, no moral, no causes, no effects." But the burden of Vonnegut's first chapter is that to do so would be to deny one's humanity. Vonnegut can't deny that he is an Earthling who must believe whatever clocks and calendars tell him. Further, he is an intelligent, sensitive Earthling who knows that from a human point of view there *are* causes and effects, not to mention morals. The effects of Dresden are terrible but they can be reckoned. The effects of helping other Earthlings are also real, so Vonnegut can remark that it is "a lovely thing" for Mary O'Hare to be a trained nurse. It is a lovely thing because it is so *human*. Vonnegut also says that he loves Lot's wife for having spurned God's rather Tralfmadorian advice. He himself has become a pillar of salt because, unlike his hero, he cannot reject the burden of being human.

It may seem that Vonnegut has contradicted himself, for Billy's "lie" apparently expresses a profoundly human need at the same time that it denies his humanity. In point of fact, the contradiction is Pilgrim's. Indeed, the pathos of Billy's story is captured in this paradox. Because he is one of those people who are in terrible trouble and not intelligent enough to get out of it, Billy is unable to imagine a saving lie except one that denies personal moral responsibility. Of course, for those who see Vonnegut as a quietist, this is as it should be. These critics see the Tralfamadorian message as an example of *foma*, or "harmless untruths," a concept advocated in an earlier Vonnegut novel, *Cat's Cradle* (1963). Whether this is indeed the case is crucial to any interpretation of the later novel.

It is true that Vonnegut follows such philosophers as Vaihinger in arguing that all human ideas are fictions. As Vonnegut once said, "everything is a lie, because our brains are two-bit computers, and we can't get very high-grade truths out of them." For this reason, man must follow Vaihinger's advice and live by his fictions as if they were "true," as if their validity could somehow be demonstrated. Man must embrace fictions that are "harmless" because their human consequences are benign. In this interview, Vonnegut went on to say that while brains are two-bit computers, "we do have the freedom to make up comforting lies." Asked for an example of a comforting lie, Vonnegut replied, " 'Thou shall not kill.' That's a good lie. Whether God said it or not, it's still a perfectly good lie."

So far as *Slaughterhouse-Five* is concerned, the question is whether the theories of Tralfamadore qualify as *foma*. In a very limited sense the answer is yes, for these theories do provide comfort for people like Billy Pilgrim. But what comforts Pilgrim will not do the job for everyone. Finally there is a great difference between the quietistic notions of Tralfamadore and the injunction not to kill. The latter is a truly comforting "lie": it implies that human life is inherently valuable, and it suggests that men are capable of *choosing* whether or not they will destroy their fellow human beings. The consequences of accepting this idea are altogether agreeable. The consequences of believing in Tralfamadore and its theories are something else again. Vonnegut is careful to show that these consequences involve more than enabling Billy Pilgrim to achieve a sustaining serenity. They involve an indifference to moral problems which is the ultimate "cause" of events like Dresden.

Critics of *Slaughterhouse-Five* seem never to notice that it is filled with Tralfamadorians who look very much like human beings. An obvious example would be the German guards who brutalize Billy Pilgrim and his fellow prisoners of war. The connection with Tralfamadorian fatalism is suggested by an interesting parallel. When he is kidnapped by the Tralfamadorians, Billy inquires of his captors, "Why me?" The Tralfamadorians reply, "Why you? Why *us* for that matter? Why *anything*?" Later, one of Billy's fellow prisoners is beaten gratuitously by a German guard. "Why me?" the prisoner asks. "Vy you? Vy anybody?" the guard answers. This parallel exposes the inhumane consequences of adopting the Tralfamadorian point of view, for the denial of personal responsibility easily leads to the brutal excesses of the Nazis. Vonnegut hardly sees the problem as peculiarly Germanic, however. Early in chapter one, he reminisces about his experiences as a police reporter for the Chicago City News Bureau. One day he covered the death of a young veteran who had been squashed in a freak elevator accident. The woman writer who took his report calmly asked him to contact the dead man's wife and pretend to be a police captain. He was to do this in order to get her response. As Vonnegut remarks, "World War II had certainly made everybody very tough." This sort of complacence might be termed quasi-Tralfamadorian. What is missing is an attempt to rationalize the status quo. This comes later from a Marine major at a Lions Club meeting: "He said that Americans had no choice but to keep fighting in Vietnam until they achieved victory or until the Communists realized that they could not force their way of life on weak countries." It seems that America had "no choice" but to remain in Vietnam. But then the Allies had no choice but to destroy Dresden, either, or so Billy is told by Bertram Copeland Rumfoord, a retired brigadier general in the Air Force Reserve and the official Air Force historian. "It *had* to be done," Rumfoord tells Billy. "Pity the men who had to *do* it." Billy assures Rumfoord that he understands: "Everything is all right, and everybody has to do exactly what he does. I learned that on Tralfamadore." As this reply suggests, Rumfoord's statements are in the best spirit of Tralfamadore. The general has obviously read his Pope: Whatever is, is right.

The scene involving Rumfoord and Billy Pilgrim is positioned at the end of *Slaughterhouse-Five* because it is the real climax to Vonnegut's complex protest novel. The object of satiric attack turns out to be a complacent response to the horrors of the age. The horror of Dresden is not just that it *could* happen here, in an enlightened twentieth century. The real horror is that events such as Dresden continue to occur and no one seems appalled. *Slaughterhouse-Five* is filled with allusions to such postwar disasters as Vietnam, the assassinations of Bobby Kennedy and Martin Luther King, Jr., and the riots in American ghettos. Vonnegut stresses the kinship between these events and Dresden, most notably in the scene where Billy Pilgrim drives his Cadillac through a burned-down ghetto which reminds him "of some of the towns he had seen in the war." These are the problems Billy avoids in his life as Lions Club President, Tastee-Freeze entrepreneur, and Reagan supporter. These are the problems the Marine major and Professor Rumfoord would see as "inevitable." But it is one thing to say that human problems are insoluble if one has visited Tralfamadore. It is quite another to support this view from a strictly Earthling perspective. Vonnegut's point is that insofar as men are guided by the likes of Professor Rumfoord, they act as if the Tralfamadorians were real and their deterministic assumptions valid. Yet Rumfoord's assertion that Dresden *had* to be is obviously false. The distinguishing feature of the raid on Dresden is that there was no strategic advantage to it whatsoever. The assertion is not a true example of *foma* because the notion of harmless untruths implies that there are also *harmful* untruths. Man must judge his lies by their consequences, and the consequences are disastrous if people in power believe that Dresden was inevitable. In Vonnegut's view, the consequences are Vietnam, the ghettos, and a social order that seriously considers the election of Ronald Reagan as President of the United States.

What Vonnegut has done in *Slaughterhouse-Five* is "poison" his readers with humanity. The term is his own:

> And it's been the university experience that taught me that there is a very good reason that you catch people before they become generals and presidents and so forth and you poison their minds with . . . humanity, and however you want to poison their minds, it's presumably to encourage them to make a better world.

Vonnegut is not sanguine about the possibilities for this better world, for he believes that the people in power really determine the quality of life in any age. As he once told the graduating class at Bennington, "Another great swindle is that people your age are supposed to save the world. . . . It isn't up to you. You don't have the money and the power. . . . It is up to older people to save the world." Alas, the older people seem to respect men like Professor

Rumfoord. Yet the effort can and must be made to "poison" the young with more humane values.

Vonnegut's Bennington speech has been grossly misrepresented by those who would characterize him as a quietist. Glen Meeter, for example, cites the passage just quoted as proof that Vonnegut is a Tralfamadorian at heart. In doing so, Meeter ignores what Vonnegut went on to tell the Bennington graduates: "When it really is time for you to save the world, when you have some power and know your way around, when people can't mock you for looking so young, I suggest that you work for a socialist form of government." He ignores Vonnegut's blunt rejection of the Tralfamadorian view of man: "Military science is probably right about the contemptibility of man in the vastness of the universe. Still—I deny that contemptibility, and I beg you to deny it."

Slaughterhouse-Five presents much the same argument. The book suggests that if there is any philosophical basis to the actions of men like Professor Rumfoord, it is a callous Social Darwinism. In this spirit Rumfoord tells his doctors "that people who were weak deserved to die." But the doctors disagree, for they are "devoted to the idea that weak people should be helped as much as possible." Vonnegut is devoted to the same idea. He has said again and again that whatever man's limitations he does have the power to change the conditions of human life. *Slaughterhouse-Five* defends this position so eloquently because it blinks at none of the attendant problems. Vonnegut's self-portrait is again crucial, for the depression he acknowledges in his own history testifies to the terrible effort men must make if they would commit themselves to an all but impossible task. No one knows better than Vonnegut that the vast majority of comforting lies are insufficient. He has recently redefined *foma* as "harmless untruths, intended to comfort simple souls. An example: 'Prosperity is just around the corner.'" It will take more than this sort of thing to defeat the "bad" illusions of Marine majors and Air Force historians. But for those who are not such simple souls, the alternative to concerted action is suicide.

Vonnegut's next novel, *Breakfast of Champions*, is about an unsimple soul named Kurt Vonnegut who does contemplate suicide as a viable option. It is about a man who seriously entertains the Tralfamadorian view of man as machine, who has "come to the conclusion that there was nothing sacred about myself or about any human being, that we were all machines, doomed to collide and collide and collide." It is a novel about a man who is "rescued" from this philosophical cul-de-sac by the assertion of one of his characters that most of man's parts may be "dead machinery," but there is still "an unwavering band of light" in man, his human *awareness*, which must be seen as sacred. Other men must see it this way, too, for as Vonnegut says,

". . . there is no order to the world around us. . . . We must adapt ourselves to the requirements of chaos instead." Having so adapted himself, Vonnegut can say, in the subtitle to *Breakfast of Champions*, "Goodbye Blue Monday!" This assertion is dramatically unimpressive, but it does suggest that the author of *Slaughterhouse-Five* knows very well that the requirements of chaos demand human vigilance and not "resigned acceptance." Indeed, they demand the insistence on humane practices which is the burden of everything Vonnegut has written.

LAWRENCE R. BROER

Slaughterhouse-Five: *Pilgrim's Progress*

From *Player Piano* to *Slaughterhouse-Five* Vonnegut describes the "collisions" of people and machinery without apparent resolution—an expression of the author's own state of mind as he attempts to work out the schizophrenic dilemma of his major characters. In *Breakfast of Champions* (1973) Vonnegut tells us that the idea of schizophrenia had fascinated him for years. "I did not and do not know for certain that I have that disease," he says. "I was sick for awhile, though. I am better now. Word of honor—I am better now." In a lighter vein, Vonnegut portrays his personal disequilibrium in reference to what he calls "Hunter Thompson's disease"—the affliction of "all those who feel that Americans can be as easily led to beauty as to ugliness, to truth as to public relations, to joy as to bitterness. . . . I don't have it this morning. It comes and it goes." So come and go the efforts of Malachi Constant, Howard Campbell, Jonah, and Eliot Rosewater to overcome that fear, cynicism, and will-lessness which impedes the spiritual growth of Vonnegut's hero.

Each of these characters is more successful, however, than Paul Proteus in achieving moral awareness and combining this awareness with existential responsibility for his actions. Each confronts the dark side of his personality and attempts to practice the moral imperative described by Malachi's spiritual twin, Unk, in *Sirens of Titan* as, "making war against the core of his

From *Sanity Plea: Schizophrenia in the Novels of Kurt Vonnegut.* © 1989 by Lawrence R. Broer.

being, against the very nature of being a machine." Yet, tormented by the fear that he is no better than a robot in a machine-dominated world, each moves back from the threshold of complete moral awakening. The lingering pessimism that is Kilgore Trout, or Billy Pilgrim, remains. No resolutions are possible for Vonnegut or his protagonists until Vonnegut has found some way to achieve an "equilibrium" based on the belief that people can successfully resist becoming appendages to machines or, as is said of Billy Pilgrim and people in general in *Slaughterhouse-Five*, "the listless playthings of enormous forces."

In opposing the standard view of Vonnegut as fatalist, Kathryn Hume objects as well to the notion that Vonnegut's work is static or repetitious—repeating rather then developing, as Charles Samuels says. Hume sees that Vonnegut's "heavy reliance upon projection makes his books unusually interdependent," "a single tapestry." She infers the spiritual progress of Paul Proteus by noting "the artistic and personal problems he [Vonnegut] takes up in one story are directly affected by those he did or did not solve in the previous story." Nowhere is Hume's insistence upon the intensely personal nature of Vonnegut's work and upon continuity and progress at the heart of Vonnegut's vision more pertinent than in the case of *Slaughterhouse-Five* and *Breakfast of Champions*—novels that Vonnegut says were conceived as one book and that Peter Reed identifies as the "central traumatic, revelatory, and symbolic moment" of Vonnegut's career.

A striking paradox of *Slaughterhouse-Five* is that it presents us with Vonnegut's most completely demoralized protagonist while making what is to this point the most affirmative statement of Vonnegut's career. The former heroes' gains in awareness and moral courage fail Billy Pilgrim entirely—by design—for Billy like Kilgore Trout in *Breakfast of Champions* becomes Vonnegut's scapegoat, carrying the author's heaviest burden of trauma and despair, but his sacrifice makes possible Vonnegut's own "rebirth." Vonnegut is careful to dissociate himself from Billy as from no character before—signaled by the fact that the author speaks to us directly in the important first chapter about the impact of the war on him, and that with references such as "I was there," and "that was me," he personally turns up in the narrative four times.

To understand that personal catharsis is central to Vonnegut's intentions, one must appreciate Thomas Wymer's view of those ludicrous-looking extraterrestrials in *Sirens of Titan* and *Slaughterhouse-Five* who kidnap Billy Pilgrim and appear to teach him wonderful ways to cope with suffering and death. Disputing the usual interpretation that the Tralfamadorians speak for the author, Wymer shows that Vonnegut warns *against* the perils of fatalism rather than affirms such a philosophy. Those who confuse Vonnegut with Billy Pilgrim or mistake the author as a defeatist, believing that the insidiously addictive ideas that come to invade Billy's mind are Vonnegut's miss the predominantly affirmative thrust of *Slaughterhouse-Five* and Vonnegut's career as a whole. Billy Pilgrim's conversion to Tralfamadorian fatalism, OR FATAL DREAM, which is Tralfamadore by anagram, assures his schizophrenic descent into madness.

It is not surprising that readers typically confuse Tralfamadorian pessimism with the author's own thinking. Doubtlessly the author breathes some of his own despair into the dazed, impotent, and demoralized Billy Pilgrim. In an address at Bennington College in 1970, the author said:

> I thought scientists were going to find out exactly how everything worked and then make it work better. I fully expected that by the time I was twenty-one, some scientists, maybe my brother, would have taken a color photograph of God Almighty and sold it to *Popular Mechanics* magazine. What actually happened when I was twenty-one was that we dropped scientific truth on Hiroshima.

At the end of World War II, while serving as a prisoner of war in Dresden, Germany, Kurt Vonnegut had scientific truth of this kind dropped on him as well, a truth that killed one hundred thirty-five thousand people and metamorphosed the loveliest city he had ever seen, "intricate and voluptuous and enchanted . . . into a blackened, smoldering hole." In fact it is to pour out his personal pessimism about the massacre machinery of war and about the lasting traumatic effects of the war on his nerves that Vonnegut writes the important autobiographical first chapter of *Slaughterhouse-Five*.

While Vonnegut comments about the ineffectiveness of war protests, the antiwar element in this novel is direct and powerful. Vonnegut tells his sons not to work for companies that make war machinery and to express contempt for people who think we need machinery like that. Vonnegut makes clear that it is *O'Hare*'s view that antiwar books are like antiglacier books. True to his promise to O'Hare's wife, Vonnegut demonstrates that wars are fought by children, subtitling his novel "The Children's Crusade"; characters who glorify war like Colonel Wild Bob and Bertram Copeland Rumfoord are made to appear absolutely ridiculous. In one telling image, a war movie run in reverse, Vonnegut demonstrates the power of art to subvert the destructive process of war. Fires go out; dead or wounded soldiers are made whole; bombs fly back into planes which fly backwards to friendly cities; the bombers are dismantled and minerals used for bombs are returned to the earth. Unfortunately, Billy uses fantasy not to reconstruct his own robotic personality, but to escape the present. His vision transports him to an

Edenic world of "two perfect people named Adam and Eve." He seeks a
condition of "pre-birth."

Billy Pilgrim's gentleness and subsequent refusal to participate in the
world's destructiveness elicits our sympathy. Richard Erlich notes that even
Billy's virtue as a "fool among knaves" [from Swift's *Tale of a Tub*] is a laudable
ideal. We see Billy as a latterday Christ who spends three days entombed in
a slaughterhouse/bomb shelter. On the way to his Dresden prison camp,
Billy suffers a sleepless agony, clinging to a "cross-brace"; he is found "lying
at an angle on the corner-brace, self crucified." Yet Billy is every bit as
"flamboyantly sick" as Eliot Rosewater, who joins Billy in a mental ward.
What passes for gentleness indicates the lobotomy performed on Billy by the
cruel conditions around him. Billy is so crippled by the psychologically
damaging blows he receives before, during, and after the war that he
increasingly withdraws from reality and ultimately loses his sanity.
Suggesting the spiritual death that awaits him, he arises from his
underground tomb to find a green coffin and an old man pushing a baby
carriage. Billy's retreat from pain into the "morphine paradise" of
Tralfamadore (whose inhabitants are green) will cancel any hope of new life.

The horrors of Dresden, Hiroshima, Nagasaki, and the Nazi
concentration camps focus the panorama of violence and inhumanity that
defines Pilgrim's world. Death, senseless cruelty, and absurd injustice are
Vonnegut's main subject, prompting him to say that, "I believe . . . even if wars
didn't keep coming like glaciers, there would still be plain old death." Thus the
slaughterhouse where Billy is kept as a prisoner in Dresden becomes more
than a grotesque naturalistic image of human beings dehumanized by war,
hanging like butchered animals on hooks. It becomes an all-encompassing
metaphor for human existence in which suffering and death are commonplace.
"So it goes," says Billy Pilgrim, without relief, cessation, or sense, now as
always.

If one counts deaths that are predicted or imagined as well as those that
occur, there may be a greater proliferation of corpses in *Slaughterhouse-Five*
than in any other twentieth-century novel. We encounter death by
starvation, rotting, incineration, squashing, gassing, shooting, poisoning,
bombing, torturing, hanging, and relatively routine death by disease. We get
the deaths of dogs, horses, pigs, Vietnamese soldiers, crusaders, hunters,
priests, officers, hobos, actresses, prison guards, a slave laborer, a suffragette,
Jesus Christ, Robert Kennedy, Martin Luther King, Billy Pilgrim's mother
and father, his wife, Edgar Derby, Roland Weary, the regimental chaplain's
assistant, Paul Lazzaro, Colonel Wild Bob; we get the deaths of a bottle of
champagne, billions of body lice, bacteria, and fleas; the novel; entire towns,
and finally the universe; we encounter individual deaths; the death of groups

en masse; accidental, calculated, and vengeful deaths; recent and historical deaths. So it goes, says Billy Pilgrim, in a world of senseless suffering and meaningless death.

There may be hundreds of "corpse mines" operating in Dresden, but through Billy's time travelling we see that his entire life is like a corpse mine—a continuity of terror stretching all the way back to childhood when his hairy father threw him in the pool at the Y.M.C.A. and told him to sink or swim (which he says was "like an execution"—Derby's?) and forward in time to his death when Paul Lazzaro makes good his promise to have Billy killed after the war. At age twelve Billy wets his pants when from the "rim of Bright Angel Point," his parents make him peer into the cavernous depths of the Grand Canyon. The place is notorious for suicidal leaps. The vortex of Carlsbad Caverns, whose "darkness . . . was total" proves equally frightening. We hear that Billy's parents have placed a particularly gruesome crucifix on the wall of his bedroom, hence that Billy "had contemplated torture and hideous wounds at the beginning and the end of nearly every day of his childhood." Billy responds to childhood trauma as much as to the horrors of war when he commits himself to a mental hospital during his senior year at the Ilium School of Optometry. Billy feels that his mother's presence at his hospital bedside is particularly threatening. He feels himself get "much sicker" and pulls the covers over his head until she goes away. He experiences schizophrenic disorientation at the sight of her lipstick-smeared cigarettes and the "dead water" on the bedside table. Billy recoils from his mother because she is insipid, materialistic, and morally obtuse, but he is mystified that his aversion, his embarrassment and weakness in her presence, should be so strong simply because she gave him life.

Billy fails to associate fears of his father's aggression (throwing him into the deep end of the Y.M.C.A. swimming pool, then taking him to the rim of the Grand Canyon) with Oedipal desire for his mother conveyed by the womb/vortex imagery of rims and dark, foreboding holes. It is notably at his mother's touch that Billy wets himself. Montana Wildhack, a surrogate mother in Billy's Tralfamadorian fantasy, later causes Billy to have wet dreams. Billy and Eliot Rosewater share a mental ward partly because of what they had seen in war, but also because neither has yet penetrated that Oedipal screen Eliot's doctor describes as "the most massively defended neurosis I've ever attempted to treat." In the most direct and intimate Oedipal fantasy in all Vonnegut's fiction, Billy longs for the peace and security he felt during infant bathings:

> Billy zoomed back in time to his infancy. He was a baby who had just been bathed by his mother. Now his mother wrapped him in

a towel, carried him into a rosy room that was filled with sunshine. She unwrapped him, laid him on the tickling towel, powdered him between the legs, joked with him, patted his little jelly belly. Her palm on his little jelly belly made potching sounds.

Billy gurgled and cooed.

Eliot is right when he comments to Billy's mother, "a boy *needs* a father." But Billy's father is dead and the alienation between Eliot and Senator Rosewater appears irremediable. Only when Vonnegut's repressed persona begins to deal with buried Oedipal tensions and asserts a creative, independent identity will he stop being "dead to the world," masking his fears with escapist fantasies or drugging himself to reality. John Tilton rightly observes that life against death-in-life is the psychic conflict at the core of this novel. In Billy, the conflict between Eros and Thanatos significantly intensifies. The inability to bring repressed fear and guilt to consciousness causes Billy to pervert that which is organic and procreative (the vagina) into that which is mechanical and destructive, an entrapping mechanistic spiral. Not only must Billy deal with normal Oedipal longings; he must reconcile himself to a mother whose coldness and insensitivity to his feelings deepens his guilt and insecurity.

Vonnegut's omnipresent "clock" effectively merges Billy's childhood nightmare with that of his war experience—"the greatest massacre in European history, which was the fire-bombing of Dresden." In the darkness (literal and metaphorical) of Carlsbad Caverns, the sudden glare of his father's pocket watch transports Billy forward in time to World War II. According to the Tralfamadorians, the two "clumps" of time bear no connection—"no moral, no causes, no effects." Not only is time meaningless; they say the universal clock is fixed, immutable, and immune to human intervention. Events are inevitably structured to be the way they are and hence do not lend themselves to warnings or explanations. Only on earth is freedom of will a subject to be taken seriously. Lulled by the Tralfamadorian "anesthetic" of fatalism, Billy remains a "bug trapped in amber," a moral sleep walker who substitutes forms of "morphine paradise" for necessary self-analysis. Billy's moral paralysis makes him feel as if he is "frozen," turned to "stone," entrapped by the spirallike ladder that leads into the Tralfamadorian spaceship. Will-less and unaware, he fails to see that his father's unconscious hostility, the violence of lunatic nations at war, Tralfamadorian aggression, and his own passivity represent the same universal will to destruction.

Nothing really prepares Billy Pilgrim for the momentous horrors of Dresden and the unimaginable displays of human cruelty and injustice offered by the war. It is not long after Billy is sent overseas that he develops a vivid sense of the monstrous torture instruments, the killing machines of war, that tear and mutilate the body and create such sadistic creatures as the revenge-crazed Paul Lazzaro, who carries a list in his head of people he is going to have killed after the war, and the equally rabid Roland Weary. Billy learns from Weary about wounds that won't heal, about "blood gutters" and such tortures as having your head drilled through with a dentist's drill and being staked to an anthill in the desert.

Billy's natural gentleness and innocence, appropriate to his role as a chaplain's assistant, hardly prepare him for the idiocy of battle. Vonnegut writes,

> Weary was as new to war as Billy. He was a replacement, too. As a part of a gun crew, he had helped to fire one shot in anger— from a 57-millimeter antitank gun. The gun made a ripping sound like the opening of the zipper on the fly of God Almighty. The gun lapped up snow and vegetation with a blowtorch thirty feet long. . . . It killed everybody on the gun crew but Weary.

In Billy's mind, war has converted the creative potency of God Almighty, along with his own, to aggression and death. Billy is loath to discover that his wife associates sex and glamor with war. In the opening chapter, Vonnegut jokes that the war has made his own phallus inoperable—a "tool" that "won't pee anymore." Billy's prisoner-of-war experience becomes an "acrimonious madrigal," a nightmare of victimization and madness. He and everyone around him exhibit some form of insane, mechanically conditioned behavior, that which is overtly aggressive, or that which allows aggression to happen. On the one hand, we encounter the mindless hating and killing, superpatriot machines of Howard Campbell, Colonel Wild Bob, and Bertram Copeland Rumfoord, whose glorifications of war and exhortations to battle appear ludicrous alongside the pitiful suffering of Billy and his comrades. Billy himself looks like "a broken kite." Billy's absorption in the prison-camp production of Cinderella confirms his schizophrenic deterioration. He can relate only to imaginary scenes and people. "Theatrical grief" becomes more real to him than anything in the outside world. Cinderella's silver boots, he discovers, fit him perfectly—"Billy Pilgrim was Cinderella, and Cinderella was Billy Pilgrim." Billy even has to be told that he has caught fire standing too close to a prison-camp stove, an alarm as foreboding as the "enormous clock" that presides over the Cinderella set and the "sea" of dying Russian prisoners in which Billy finds himself "dead-center." No wonder, then, that Billy's self-protective delusions lead him to dream, like Eliot Rosewater, of floating up "among the treetops," or, like Malachi Constant, to hallucinate a "morphine paradise" such as Tralfamadore. Either prospect leaves him as disembodied as Winston Niles Rumfoord in *Sirens of Titan*. Notably, the Hound of Space, Kazak, barks in a voice "like a big bronze gong."

We encounter the equally mindless cheerfulness of the British prisoners of war, whose obsessive pretense of order and cleanliness causes them to put up a sign that reads, "Please leave this latrine as tidy as you found it," a madness of its own. This form of hopeless programming includes illusions of peace and harmony of people like Billy's wife and mother, who are blind to the more sordid and desperate aspects of existence, and the awkward sentimentality and automatic loyalty to God and country of Edgar Derby. All are fully automated boobs, ready to conform to the most convenient mold, whether in the mistaken interests of survival or friendliness or out of the lack of imagination to do anything better; thus, they become the ready slaves of whatever anonymous bureaucracies, computers, or authoritarian institutions take hold of their minds.

The horrors of war that prove most traumatic of all to Billy are the destruction of Dresden and the death of his best friend, Edgar Derby. Billy had been told by the English prisoners of war that, "You needn't worry about bombs, by the way . . . Dresden is an open city. It is undefended, and contains no war industries or troop concentrations of any importance." Despite his manly bluff and awkward sentimentality, Derby seems a symbolic human extension of Dresden. He is a teacher of Contemporary Civilization who enters the war out of pure motives, who takes care of his body, and who with utter sincerity, over the rude suggestion of Paul Lazzaro that he "go take a flying fuck at the moon," tries to provide helpful leadership to Billy and his fellow prisoners. Derby's loyalty to the sacred, civilized graces of family, love, God, country, leads Billy to believe that Derby must be the greatest father in the world. Yet none of this exempts Derby from the stupidity and absurdity of death, which Vonnegut himself comments upon in the first chapter of the book:

> I think the climax of the book will be the execution of poor old Edgar Derby. . . . The irony is so great. A whole city gets burned down, and thousands and thousands of people are killed. And then this one American foot soldier is arrested in the ruins for taking a teapot. And he's given a regular trial, and then shot by a firing squad.

Other pitiful ironies of war that wear indelibly on Billy are the execution of Private Eddie Slovik, shot for challenging authority, and the fact that despite all the popular movies that glorify war and soldiering starring manly figures like John Wayne or Frank Sinatra, it is usually the nation's young and innocent who are first sent to be slaughtered.

Life for Billy after the war seems no less brutal or pointless; like glaciers, death keeps right on coming. All the members of Billy's family suffer hideous deaths, his wife by carbon monoxide poisoning, his father in a hunting accident, and everybody on the plane flying to an optometrists' convention is killed in a crash, except Billy and the copilot. Linking the horrors of war with the horrors of civilian life, Billy mistakes the Austrian ski instructors who come to rescue him for German soldiers. He whispers to them his address: "Slaughterhouse Five." Billy's life at home is filled with the same pain and warpedness, the same maddening contrasts between sanity and insanity that went with war. He turns on the television set only to find that all the shows are about silliness or murder. He looks into the window of a tawdry bookstore only to find hundreds of books about sexual perversion and murder. He looks up at the news of the day being written across the top of a building and finds it to be about power, anger, and death.

Vonnegut protests the literal holes machines put in people, but it is the more subtle, spiritually corrosive effects of technological progress that destroy Billy's equilibrium for good. Surrounded by the soulless junk of middle-class suburbia and saddled with an inane wife who can't believe anyone has married her, Billy leads a sterile, machine-ridden life. In robot fashion, all sixty-eight thousand employees of General Forge and Foundry Company in Ilium are required to wear safety glasses manufactured by their own firm. "Frames are where the money is," Vonnegut remarks. Billy lives in an all-electric home, sleeps in a bed with Magic Fingers, owns a fifth of a Holiday Inn, and half of three Tastee-Freeze stands. In a perfectly chosen image of the debasement of spiritual realities by machinery, Vonnegut has Billy playing hymns on an organ and sermonizing from a portable altar made by a vacuum cleaner company in Camden, New Jersey. Not only has Billy's mechanical world despiritualized his environment and traumatized him with its awesome power for physical destruction; it has depleted his imagination and his will to be something better than a machine himself.

Is it really any wonder that Billy Pilgrim learns to experience death as merely a "violet light and a hum," and that he invents a pain-killing philosophy of life for refuge? Whether it is the horrors of the Dresden holocaust or the nightmare of Billy's vapid civilian life at home with a fat and inane wife, what finally destroys Billy's equilibrium is the irreconcilable contrast in his life between an ideal world of beauty, justice, mercy, and peace, and that of the psychologically devastating accumulation of horrors that turn him into a dazed and disembodied scarecrow. This principle of ironic contrast—between Dresden and holocaust, justice and the arbitrary death of Edgar Derby—separates. Billy from his sanity, inducing that state of "catalepsis" that lands Eliot Rosewater in an asylum.

Billy's final unbalancing, equal to Eliot Rosewater's "big click," comes at Billy's and Valencia's anniversary party when Billy listens to a barbershop quartet. Vonnegut writes:

> As the quartet made slow, agonized experiments with chords— chords intentionally sour, sourer still, unbearably sour, and then a chord that was suffocatingly sweet, and then some sour ones again . . . Billy had powerful psychosomatic responses to the changing chords. His mouth filled with the taste of lemonade, and his face became grotesque, as though he really were being stretched on the torture engine called the rack.

Psychosomatic responses, indeed. Life, with its torturous vacillation between sweet and sour, sublimity and pathos, has become so unendurable for Billy that he becomes stuporous, his actions somnambulistic, and in an act of total disengagement, he retreats "upstairs in his nice white house," which gives every appearance of being an asylum. Billy struggles momentarily to understand "the big secret somewhere inside." He remembers the night Dresden was destroyed—the firestorm that "ate everything . . . that would burn," that turned the city into a desert and people into little petrified human beings. But Billy is again incapable of bringing his nightmare into full consciousness; rather he calls upon the consolations and alleged wisdom of his outer-space, or inner-space, friends, the Tralfamadorians, who cause him to believe that death does not matter since no one really dies, hence to resign himself to his own death at the hands of Paul Lazzaro. The reality of Billy's death is problematical, more a death-wish produced by unloving parents and the horrors of war. After learning that Billy's "will" is "locked" up with the tape on which he sees his death enacted, we are told that nobody else was there—indeed, "not even Billy Pilgrim is there." Perhaps Billy is merely hallucinating again—his death no more real than those Tralfamadorian flying saucers that "come from nowhere."

According to Patrick Shaw, the key to understanding the Tralfamadorians resides in their physical attributes, described thus:

> They were two feet high, and green, and shaped like plumber's friends. Their suction cups were on the ground, and their shafts, which were extremely flexible, usually pointed to the sky. At the top of each shaft was a little hand with a green eye in its palm.

"A plumber's friend," Shaw explains,

is the common household implement consisting of a rubber suction cup attached to a broomstick-like handle. It is a gadget used for unclogging drains, for quite literally loosening excrement and accumulated filth from sewage pipes.

Therefore Shaw concludes that the Tralfamadorians perform the symbolic function for Pilgrim of cleansing the pipes of his perception, unclogging his vision and imagination by disabusing him of historical, sociological fixations. One assumes that Shaw means the belief that human beings can have a meaningful impact upon future events, that they can influence their own lives. Says Shaw, "Roland Weary tries quite literally to 'beat the living shit' out of Pilgrim, but only the Tralfamadorians, through unsentimental, sardonic logic, succeed in removing the waste from Pilgrim's mind. Himself a bit of human waste sticking in the cosmological pipes, Pilgrim comes 'unstuck in time' and simultaneously unclogs his own perceptions so that he realizes the 'negligibility of death, and the true nature of time.'"

Shaw agrees with David Goldsmith that the superior vision provided by the cycloptic Tralfamadorian eye atop the phallic, shaftlike periscope contrasts with Pilgrim's own failure as an earthly optometrist to improve the way in which people see. Billy falls asleep fitting his patients. Shaw says, "As his own vision is progressively cleared by his experiences with the spacemen, as he realizes more and more the defectiveness of his earthly 'eyes' and the fallacies of history and earth time, Pilgrim is less able to function as an eye doctor." As "one who is taught by extraterrestrial powers how to see into the past, the present, and the future," he becomes in a sense a kind of "contemporary, spastic Tiresias." Goldsmith argues that as a projection of the author's own condition, this cleansing of Billy's pipes marks Vonnegut's "mature acceptance" of the horrors of life as something it does no good to worry about. Such a perspective, says Goldsmith, "simply provides the comforts which have enabled Vonnegut to live with his wartime nightmare. Death, from the Tralfamadorian view, no matter how horrible, can have no significance." Thus Goldsmith says Vonnegut has finally washed the horror and guilt of Dresden from his mind and has come to accept the previously unacceptable—man's capacity for evil and his helplessness to do much better, as if he were controlled by some exterior force. To wit, "Billy the optometrist who fits people with glasses has fitted Vonnegut with a pair which, if not exactly rose colored, have enabled him to see things in their proper perspective."

Because of the seeming inevitability of those forces that enfeeble Billy Pilgrim's will to survive, most critics agree with Shaw and Goldsmith that Billy's weary lament, "So it goes," projects the author's own sense of futility. Yet nothing seems further from the point of Vonnegut's novel than to believe that the Tralfamadorians speak for the author—that what Stanley Kauffmann and Jack Richardson join in calling the wisdom of "a higher order of life" is in fact a revelation of the author's own sense of hopelessness in the face of those enormous deterministic forces that make playthings of all the novel's characters. Those who argue that the fatalistic philosophy offered by the Tralfamadorians makes *Slaughterhouse-Five* seem full of danger are right. The consolations of Tralfamadorian fatalism are hideously bobby trapped—leading to a form of moral paralysis that precludes responsibility or action. Billy's flight from the responsibilities of "wakeful humanity" leads directly into what John Tilton calls "a spiritual oubliette."

Not only do the Tralfamadorians, with their "earthly combination of ferocity and spectacular weaponry and talent for horror" not improve Billy's vision, they eventually blow up the universe while experimenting with new fuels for flying saucers. Caged in a zoo, turned into a puppet and made to do the bidding of mechanical creatures whose own world is both physically and morally sterile, Billy in his tranquilized existence becomes the very embodiment of what Vonnegut has warned against for years. Insulated from pain, Billy has simply abdicated his humanity, trading his dignity and self-integrity for an illusion of comfort and security, and becoming himself a machine.

If settling into his womblike Tralfamadorian environment, closing his eyes to any unpleasantness in the world, Billy Pilgrim becomes more than ever the plaything of those enormous forces at work on him throughout his life, Kurt Vonnegut may have saved his own sanity through the therapeutic processes of art, climaxed by an act of symbolic amputation: the severing of the Billy Pilgrim within himself, poisoned with existential gangrene. That this is as much Kurt Vonnegut's baptism by fire as it is the story of Billy's madness may be the overriding truth of *Slaughterhouse-Five;* hence, the revelation in *Breakfast of Champions* that, "I see a man who is terribly wounded, because he has dared to pass through the fires of truth to the other side, which we have never seen. And then he has come back again to tell us about the other side." Billy's regress is Vonnegut's progress. Not only has Vonnegut shored up his own sanity by facing directly into the fires of Dresden, making his long-deferred "dance with death," without which he says no art is possible, but like Lot's wife he has asserted his inviolable humanity and freed himself from the self-imprisoning fatalism of Tralfamadore. Vonnegut knows that the Tralfamadorians are merely ourselves—an appropriate symbol for the mechanistic insanity of our own planet, an extension into the future of our own warlike globe. He knows too that with sufficient imagination and heart, we can, like Salo in *Sirens of Titan*, dismantle our own self-imprisoning machinery and become whatever we choose to become.

No wonder after completing this process of cleansing and renewal Vonnegut said,

> Well, I felt after I finished *Slaughterhouse-Five* that I didn't have to write at all anymore if I didn't want to. . . . I suppose that flowers, when they're through blooming, have some sort of awareness of some purpose having been served. . . . At the end of *Slaughterhouse-Five* I had the feeling that I had produced this blossom. . . . that I had done what I was supposed to do and everything was O.K.

If Vonnegut's "therapy" culminates in *Slaughterhouse-Five*, the full meaning of that therapy becomes clear in a novel that not only incorporates all the essential machine themes of his previous works but which serves as nothing less than the spiritual climax to his life and career, *Breakfast of Champions*.

LEONARD MUSTAZZA

Adam and Eve in the Golden Depths: *Edenic Madness in* Slaughterhouse-Five

Critics of *Slaughterhouse-Five* have long recognized Billy Pilgrim's need to "create," albeit involuntarily, his Tralfamadorian experience. Wayne McGinnis writes that "what makes self-renewal possible in *Slaughterhouse-Five* is the human imagination, . . . the value of the mental construct." "Tralfamadore is a fantasy," argue Robert Merrill and Peter Scholl, "a desperate attempt to rationalize chaos, but one must sympathize with Billy's need to create Tralfamadore. After all, the need for supreme fictions is a very human trait." More specifically, a few commentators have noticed (mostly in passing) that Billy's space fantasy reflects Edenic yearnings. Frederick Karl, for instance, calls Billy's fantasy "sentimentalized, a golden age, the Edenic place, all to give Billy an alternative experience." Along somewhat different lines, Glenn Meeter argues that Billy's backward movie, which ends with Adam and Eve in Eden, reflects a vision of history as sin and shows that "the fall of man for Vonnegut is a fall from timelessness into history, as it is in heretical readings of *Paradise Lost*." Others have made similar points.

In this chapter, I would like to look closely at the linkage that Vonnegut draws in this, his most successful novel, between Eden and Tralfamadore. From the moment he comes "unstuck in time," Billy Pilgrim tries to construct for himself an Edenic experience out of materials he garners over the course of some twenty years. Although Billy's Eden differs very much

From *Forever Pursuing Genesis: The Myth of Eden in the Novels of Kurt Vonnegut.* © 1990 by Associated University Presses, Inc.

from Paul Proteus's, Malachi Constant's, and Howard Campbell's, Vonnegut subtly manipulates here the same familiar myth; and ironically, the pathetic protagonist of *Slaughterhouse-Five* is the most successful of his central figures in realizing his pursuit of Genesis. In order to throw the contours of this myth into sharper relief, I will use here not the Genesis account, for, in itself, it is far too underdeveloped. Instead, Milton's *Paradise Lost* provides a useful framework within which to consider Billy's myth, which, like Milton's Edenic sequences, reflects universal preoccupations with such matters as life and death, free will, the acquisition of knowledge, the fall into history, and the narrative recapturing of the perfect place where all answers are available, where everything is neatly ordered. Milton's epic provides a convenient and remarkably revealing exostructure against which we might compare Billy's Edenic yearnings.

It soon becomes quite clear in *Slaughterhouse-Five* that Billy Pilgrim's madness is one with a method in it: his "trip" to Tralfamadore and the "knowledge" he brings back reflecting his own desperate yearnings after peace, love, immutability, stability, and an ordered existence. To come to terms with the horrors he has witnessed in the war, Billy, taking his cue from the well-known Eliot Rosewater, his fellow patient at a veterans' hospital, tries to "re-invent [himself] and [his] universe," in which reinvention "science fiction was a big help." It comes as no surprise, of course, that the writer Rosewater recommends to Billy is none other than Kilgore Trout, whose fanciful plots, supplemented by some other outside details, help Billy to forge his illusory trip into outer space. That trip proves to be mythic in that, like traditional mythic narratives, it provides answers, decidedly idiosyncratic ones, to the existential problems confronting humanity. Joseph Campbell's distinction between myth and dream can well apply in Billy's case. Campbell defines *dream* as "personalized myth" and *myth* as "depersonalized dream," the former "quirked by the peculiar troubles of the dreamer," the latter making problems and solutions valid for all of humanity. One might fairly easily substitute *madness* for Campbell's *dream*. Like the dreamer's involuntary nightly visions, the schizophrenic's involuntary hallucinations obliquely reflect his or her own peculiar troubles. Unlike the dreamer, however, the schizophrenic cannot readily awaken and allow reality to take control, and so it is with Billy. His hallucinations must, therefore, become his reality, making him a permanent dreamer. Unlike the dreamer, too, Billy will not leave his "personalized myth" on the personal level. Rather, he depersonalizes it and tries to make it valid for everyone by sharing it on a New York radio program. In a very limited sense, what also depersonalizes his story is the fact that we can discern in it some familiar contours of other mythic narratives; and the fact that he uses the science fiction form, which Northrop Frye, among others, has associated with earlier mythic narratives, calling it "a mode of romance with a strong inherent tendency to myth." Thus, Vonnegut brilliantly turns Billy's self-generated truths into both a schizophrenic delusion and an age-old universal means of coming to terms with life's hidden meanings. As such, he also adapts this very human need for supreme fictions to the sad circumstances of Billy's life while making a wry comment on the persistence of such fictions.

The specific connection between the Tralfamadorian experience and the myth of Eden occurs subtly but unmistakably. Shortly after Billy comes "unstuck in time" during the war, he and his unwilling companion (and now would-be murderer), Roland Weary, are taken prisoner by a group of misfit German soldiers, one of whom, a middle-aged corporal, is wearing golden cavalry boots taken from a dead Hungarian soldier on the Russian front:

> Those boots were almost all he owned in this world. They were his home. An anecdote: One time a recruit was watching him bone and wax those golden boots, and he held one up to the recruit and said, "If you look in there deeply enough, you'll see Adam and Eve."
>
> Billy Pilgrim had not heard this anecdote. But, lying on the black ice there, Billy stared into the patina of the corporal's boots, saw Adam and Even in the golden depths. They were naked. They were so innocent, so vulnerable, so eager to behave decently. Billy Pilgrim loved them.

By contrast, the pair of feet next to the corporal's are swaddled in rags, and yet the imagery surrounding the owner of those feet is comparable to the mythic references used to describe the corporal's boots. Those feet belong to a fifteen-year-old boy whose face was that of a "blond angel," a "heavenly androgyne." "The boy," the narrator tells us, in a most significant analogy, "was as beautiful as Eve." What all of these images reveal is that Billy's preoccupations are rapidly moving away from the personal level toward the cosmic, from his own real and perceived experiences there on the black ice to those of the race. Shortly before Billy's capture, at the point where he becomes unstuck in time, the narrator says that "Billy's attention began to swing grandly through the full arc of his life." Specifically, he considers three pleasantly passive moments: pre-birth ("red light and bubbling sounds"), being thrown into a swimming pool by his father ("there was beautiful music everywhere"), and his own death ("violet light—and a hum"). The common thread running through these "experiences" is Billy's desire for inaction, passivity, semi-loss of consciousness, a sort of *regressus ad uterum*. When he sees Adam and Eve in the golden boots, however, his concerns are suddenly enlarged to include not only his own vulnerability to forces beyond his control, but all of humanity's, a condition that represents, mythically, a fall from Adam's and Eve's primal innocence. In other words, he begins by considering his own passive innocence and moves backwards to the innocence of the species, although, conveniently, he does not acknowledge the fact that those mythic figures in the golden depths were themselves far from passive, and that their "activity" is what is said to have caused the dire condition in which he finds himself.

Likewise, on his daughter's wedding day later in his life, Billy comes "slightly unstuck in time" and "watches" a war movie backwards, beginning with German planes sucking bullets out of American planes and ending with specialists whose job it is to bury the minerals with which bombs are made so that those minerals can never hurt anyone again. Significantly, however, Billy's wish-fulfilling movie, his imaginative effort, in Jerome Klinkowitz's words, "to turn things around" does not end there:

> The American fliers turned in their uniforms, became high school kids. And Hitler turned into a baby, Billy Pilgrim supposed. That wasn't in the movie. Billy was extrapolating. Everybody turned into a baby, and all humanity, without exception, conspired biologically to produce two perfect people named Adam and Eve, he supposed.

Vonnegut gives us unmistakable clues here as to the direction Billy's creative fantasies are taking. Billy's extrapolations and suppositions enable him to go well beyond the limits of the movie, and his additions to the film suggest his preoccupations not merely with the state of individual "babyhood," but with the innocent perfection of the race.

By the same token, however, Billy's delusions and extrapolations and his subsequent creation of a "solution" also suggest his awareness of the race's inability to go backwards. Knowing that the biblical past itself is unrecoverable, therefore, he uses various materials—his longings, his readings, his experiences—to forge a world, Tralfamadore, which is futuristic to all appearances but which, in effect, carries out all of the functions of the mythic world he yearns after. Billy finds what prove to be his most important source materials in a tawdry Times Square bookstore that he visits in 1968, over twenty years after the war. First he notices a Kilgore Trout novel entitled *The Big Board*, which concerns an Earthling couple who have been kidnapped by extraterrestrials and put on display in a zoo. The visitors to this zoo are entertained by the Earthlings' reactions to the rising and falling prices of their supposed investments on Earth. In reality, however, the telephone, the big board, and the ticker with which they monitor their "fortunes" are fakes, designed only as "stimulants to make the Earthlings perform vividly for the crowds at the zoo. . . ." In the same bookstore, Billy also sees a pornographic magazine with a question on its cover, "What really happened to Montana Wildhack?," and he subsequently watches a film on a movie machine of an erotic performance by Wildhack. All of these details, modified to suit his needs, will become quite significant in Billy's space fantasy; and Vonnegut takes pains to show whence those details derive. In this regard, the novel proves to be realistic, providing us with a portrait of a pathetic man. Yet, there is also a larger context for Billy's myth-making. His alterations to his source materials to create his personal myth again reflect his longings—as do his view of Adam and Eve in the corporal's boots in 1945 and, much later in his life, his extrapolations and suppositions about Adam and Eve while watching the backward movie. It is with these alterations that Billy is finally able to bridge the gap between his longing for Eden and the dire facts of his life. Before considering those alterations and what they imply, however, I would like to look briefly at the actions and concerns of Milton's Adam and then compare Billy's to those of the race's mythic progenitor.

Barbara Lewalski correctly observes that "in *Paradise Lost* the Edenic life is radical growth and process, a mode of life steadily increasing in complexity and challenge and difficulty but, at the same time and by that very fact, in perfection." We may best discern this increasing complexity if we consider their earliest experiences. Upon awakening to life, Adam soon realizes that he can speak; and he immediately asks "Ye Hills and Dales, ye Rivers, Woods, and Plains / And ye that live and move, fair creatures" who made him. The very act of inferring the existence of "some great Maker" from the beauty and rational order he beholds demonstrates the start of the "radical growth" that Lewalski comments upon. (It might be noted here that, in contrast to Adam's extrapolations, which lend complexity to his initial experiences, Billy's are intended to take him in the opposite direction, from horrifying complexity to simple innocence.) Before long, Adam's Maker does appear to him in "shape Divine," and gives him the "Garden of Bliss," his "Mansion," his "seat prepar'd." There Adam does two significant things: he names the creatures over which he has been given dominion, and he debates with his Maker for a mate, one in whom he can find "rational delight" and "By conversation with his like to help, / Or solace his defects." We soon learn that this debate was not so much persuasive as instructional, for God used it to observe Adam's ratiocinative powers ("for trial only brought, / To see how thou couldst judge of fit and meet") and to instruct him in disputation and reasoning. Adam, who has passed this trial admirably, is then put to sleep, and his request for a mate is granted. The result, as Adam exclaims, is magnificent:

> On she came,
> Led by her Heav'nly Maker, though unseen,
> And guided by his voice, nor uninform'd
> Of nuptial Sanctity and marriage Rites:
> Grace was in all her steps, Heav'n in her Eye,
> In every gesture dignity and love.

As always, the context in which we derive all of this information is important. Adam reveals these details in a conversation with the angel Raphael, whom Adam refers to variously as "glorious shape," "Divine instructor," "Divine Interpreter," and "Divine Historian." For his part, Raphael's function is to inform Adam about things that "surmount the reach / Of human sense," that "human sense cannot reach"; and Adam's deferential epithets reveal his awareness of the privilege conferred upon him by his angelic visitor.

Interestingly, virtually all of these elements—a prepared habitat, instruction by a higher power, a mate whom he regards as perfect—can be discerned in Billy's mythic space fantasy. Frederick Karl has noted that, "even though Billy is exhibited in a zoo, as an animal to their human, Tralfamadore represents paradise . . ." and, viewed against the background of Milton's Edenic milieu, this "paradise" comes into sharper focus.

The initial linkage of space fantasy and Eden is accomplished by Vonnegut's juxtaposing of scenes. Immediately after Billy watches his backward movie, extrapolating that the film begins/ends with Adam and Eve, he goes into the backyard to meet his Tralfamadorian kidnappers. They take him aboard their craft and introduce an anesthetic into the atmosphere so that he will sleep. When he awakens, like Adam, he finds himself in his new "Mansion," on display under a geodesic dome, the symbolic counterpart of "the uttermost convex / Of this great Round" in *Paradise Lost*. Within this domed enclosure, he breathes air. He cannot exist outside of it for the element of his transcendent masters is cyanide.

The environment in which Billy finds himself, though very different from Adam's on the surface, is also ironically comparable. The beauty of Milton's Eden is such that it fills the angels who behold it with awe, a place of stunning natural loveliness and utility, where "Out of the fertile ground [God] caus'd to grow / All Trees of noblest kind for sight, smell, taste." Billy's paradise is, likewise, a perfect place for him as a middle-class, middle-minded, twentieth-century Earthling. The natural habitat may be fine for Adam, but only the best in ornamental conveniences will do for Billy; and these come not from the hand of God but from a Sears Roebuck warehouse in Iowa City:

> There was a color television set and a couch that could be converted into a bed. There were end tables with lamps and ashtrays on them by the couch. There was a home bar and two stools. There was a little pool table. There was wall-to-wall carpeting in federal gold, except in the kitchen and bathroom areas and over the iron manhole cover in the center of the floor. There were magazines arranged in a fan on the coffee table in front of the couch.
>
> There was a stereophonic phonograph. The phonograph worked. The television didn't. There was a picture of one cowboy killing another one pasted to the television tube.

In this familiar place, Billy goes about the routines of life—eating "a good breakfast from cans," washing his plate and eating utensils, exercising, taking showers, using deodorant—and the visitors to the zoo are fascinated by his appearance and his actions. Milton's Adam and Eve are also on display to the angels, as is made clear when a disguised Satan tells Uriel that he wishes "with secret gaze, / Or open admiration" to behold the newly created beings in Eden, and when Adam tells Eve that "Millions of spiritual Creatures walk the Earth" and admire God's works, which works include the human creatures themselves. Although Milton is, of course, serious in his portrayal of the prime creatures of the new creation and the admiration they inspire in the superior spiritual beings who behold them, Vonnegut's comic portrayal nevertheless evokes a similar sense of Billy's special place in his new environment. This special status conferred (or self-conferred) on the otherwise pathetic Billy Pilgrim is further evidenced by another parallel with Adam. Like Adam in his "naked Majesty," Billy is naked in his contrived new home, and wryly evoking Adam's shameless nakedness and proud majesty, Vonnegut indicates that, since the Tralfamadorians could not know that Billy's body and face were not beautiful, "they supposed that he was a splendid specimen," and "this had a pleasant effect on Billy, who began to enjoy his body for the first time." In short, Billy has found a way to make himself like the prime of men.

By the same token, he also finds a way to make his overlords different from, and yet superior to, the weaker human species, a relationship that is also obtained in *Paradise Lost*. Although Milton's angels are invisible spirits,

Raphael takes on a form when he goes to meet Adam, and here is how the narrator describes the angel's "proper shape":

> A Seraph wing'd: six wings he wore, to shade
> His lineaments Divine; the pair that clad
> Each shoulder broad, came mantling o'er his breast
> With regal Ornament; the middle pair
> Girt like a Starry Zone his waist, and round
> Skirted his loins and thighs with downy Gold
> And colors dipt in Heav'n; the third his feet
> Shadow'd from either heel with feathered mail
> Sky-tinctur'd grain. Like *Maia's* son he stood,
> And shook his Plumes, that Heav'nly fragrance fill'd
> The circuit wide.

The divine shape (taken from Isaiah 6:2), the heavenly colors, the likening of the angel to Mercury (Maia's son) all serve to ennoble Raphael and to underscore his superior otherworldliness. Moreover, just as angels are superior to human beings in appearance, so are they above humans intellectually. Raphael soon makes clear to Adam that, while both angels and human beings have been endowed with the ability to reason, human reasoning is often carried out discursively while angels reason intuitively, the two modes "differing but in degree, of kind the same." In other words, Raphael must make certain accommodations in order to adapt the information he conveys to Adam, whose powers of comprehension are more limited than those of the angels.

Likewise, various corporeal and ratiocinative differences between human beings and Tralfamadorians are evident in *Slaughterhouse-Five*. The aliens' shape is the most humorous and provocative:

> . . . they were two feet high, and green, and shaped like plumber's friends. Their suction cups were on the ground, and their shafts, which were extremely flexible, usually pointed to the sky. At the top of each shaft was a little hand with a green eye in its palm.

Whereas Milton ennobles his "divine shapes" by making them grander than humans, Vonnegut presents the otherworldliness of the Tralfamadorians comically, simultaneously letting us share in Billy's wonder and undercutting their superiority by means of absurdity. Yet, like Milton's angels, the Tralfamadorians are far superior intellectually to their human guests. They are able to see in four dimensions, and they pity Earthlings for being able to see only in three. Moreover, like the intuitively reasoning angels, the Tralfamadorians communicate telepathically; and so, lacking voice boxes, they must make accommodations so that Billy can understand them. The accommodation here is "a computer and a sort of electric organ" to simulate human sounds. Again, Vonnegut's portrayal of these beings relies upon machinery, in this case, twentieth-century gadgets, and again, unlike Milton, he uses these familiar instruments to compel us to look from dual perspectives. From the mythic perspective, which is Billy's viewpoint, the Tralfamadorians are no more or less bizarre than the mythic shapes that people the works of Homer or Dante or Spenser, whereas, from the literal perspective, they are ridiculous. Though we might find it natural to look from this latter viewpoint, we must also acknowledge Billy's real belief in these beings. Virtually nothing is considered absurd to the true believer, and, conversely, any belief that is radically different from one's own must strike the viewer as ludicrous to some extent or other. Hence, if we judge Billy's belief from the mythic perspective, however idiosyncratic and inadequate it may be, we can sympathize with the impulse he yields to.

One final correspondence must be observed before we proceed to the more significant matter of the revelations Billy receives. As we saw, Milton's Adam, aware of his own limitations, "persuades" his creator to make a mate for him. That mate proves to be not merely a woman, but the perfect woman for Adam. Eve, on the other hand, does not see things in quite the same way initially, and so she must be brought to Adam by the creator's leading voice and, in effect, taught to love him. Similarly, Billy's fantasy involves an Eve-figure with whom he may share his Eden; and, as usual, Vonnegut both evokes the familiar myth and looks ironically at the situation by making Billy's ideal mate an erotic film star, Montana Wildhack. Like Milton's Eve, Montana is brought to Billy by their masters; like Eve, too, she initially fears her mate, but eventually learns to trust him, and they become friends and then lovers. Significantly, the narrator describes their love making as "heavenly," an adjective that is quite telling and, I think, not used casually. Finally, Billy's relationship with his mate is, like that of Milton's Adam, based not primarily on sex but on their mutual delight in conversation as evidenced by her request at one point that he tell her a story, which, not surprisingly, turns out to be one about the bombing of Dresden. In short, despite Vonnegut's joke about the kind of woman Billy sees as perfect, there is something serious, something touching, and something that partakes not at all in the stuff of erotic fantasies that one might expect from Billy's choice of women. Rather, for Billy, as for Adam, the perfection of Eden depends to a large extent upon having a partner with whom to converse and to share in the blissful state. Paradise, in other words, would be sorely lacking without a peer who is much more than a mere sex object.

These evocative surface correspondences are, however, ultimately less important than the information that Billy acquires from his sage captors, just as the information that Raphael conveys to Adam is far more important in the great scheme of things than the Edenic life itself. Indeed, in both cases, continued bliss depends upon the information conveyed, for both characters are being given a unique opportunity, in Milton's words, "to know / Of things above his World," things "which human knowledge could not reach." The things essentially concern four principal topics: free will, time, death, and the destiny of the universe. In both worlds, moreover, these issues are intimately linked, but the "answers" provided by the superior beings differ radically in each case.

Raphael's main charge is to inform Adam and Eve of the dangers that Satan poses to their happy state and of the fact that everything depends upon their exercising the right reason to bring their wills into conformity with God's singular commandment. God's charge to Raphael is explicit:

> such discourse bring on
> As may advise him of his happy state,
> Happiness in his power left free to will,
> Left to his own free will, his will though free,
> Yet mutable; whence warn him to beware
> He swerve not too secure. . . .

The emphasis upon free will and upon the direct relationship between willed action and consequence is unmistakable here, and Raphael accordingly underscores this point at every turn, even in his sociable chatter. For instance, his account of angelic modes of reasoning serves as a basis for his point that human beings can aspire to higher intellectual gifts "If ye be found obedient." He thus makes it clear that the responsibility resting upon their shoulders, though easy enough in the observance, is immense because death, the fall of the universe into corrosive time, and the fate of their descendants all hinge upon a single act of theirs.

Moving in the opposite direction from Adam, Billy Pilgrim begins from the fallen state and expresses an overwhelming desire to move symbolically backwards, going from horrid experience into a dimension where will and action are inconsequential, where time's ravenous activity is rendered unimportant, and where human destiny is in itself insignificant. Further, in forging answers to (or simply evading) the questions "where had he come from, and where should he go now?," Billy effectively "corrects" the

Edenic account so that human responsibility plays no role in the present state of affairs and the inherent nature of things obviates any concern one might have for consequences. What Tony Tanner calls Billy's "quietism" derives from the determinism with which he replaces willed and, therefore, consequential actions. In so doing, Tanner writes, Billy "abandons the worried ethical, tragical point of view of Western man and adopts a serene conscienceless passivity." To use Milton's vision again as a point of comparison, whereas the epic poet's God asserts "What I will is Fate," Billy, upon instruction from his Tralfamadorian overlords, asserts "If the accident will."

Specifically, Billy's godlike instructors tell him what he desperately wishes were true: (1) that there is no such thing as linear time, but "all moments, past, present, and future, always have existed, and always will exist"; thus, the sting of time is removed, its ability to corrode is undermined, and the tragic view that the aging process makes for is eliminated; (2) that, as a result of time's non-linear nature, no one really dies except in brief moments; (3) that, since non-linear time contains both good and bad times, one would do well to concentrate on only the good ones; (4) that there is no such thing as free will, and so human action is really irrelevant; all things happen as they must, and individuals are thus like "bugs trapped in amber"; (5) that the end of the universe is as ludicrous as its existence, the end caused not by human design or natural catastrophe, but by Tralfamadorians' testing of a new fuel. This last item is particularly suggestive, for it subtly parodies, in a Swiftian manner, the arrogance that human beings often display in our technologically dangerous time. Supposing that humankind will cause the end of life as we know it, such people reflect a kind of Lilliputian belief that we are the terrors of the universe rather than small cogs in a vast machine.

Billy himself has no such arrogant illusions except insofar as his diseased mind involuntarily makes him a form maker. "Among the things Billy Pilgrim could not change," we are told, "were the past, the present, and the future"; but, to a large extent, Billy's myth-making belies this statement. By making the alterations in the only place where they ultimately count—in his own mind—he eases the anxiety he hitherto felt. However limited, his personal myth carries out the same function that all myths do. It gives meaning to the apparently meaningless; it provides cause for hope; it affords relief from the otherwise horrible awareness of aging, death, decay, and meaningless sacrifice.

Near the end of Milton's *Paradise Lost*, the warrior angel, Michael, is sent by God both to expel Adam from paradise and to provide a preview of life in the fallen world. This preview includes many of the horrors of biblical history (for example, the murder of Abel by Cain) and the fallen natural world (for example, disease and hardship); but it also includes hopeful visions, specifically, Christ's messianic role and the possibility of salvation through willing obedience to God. Thus, Adam's view of time, though linear, is rendered complete by knowledge of the outcome—Christ's Second Coming, the resurrection of the just, and the final defeat of the evil Satanic powers. Although Billy is a Christian, he cannot bring himself to take comfort in such eschatalogical "solutions." Instead, he transforms himself into what Mircea Eliade has called "traditional man," who periodically abolishes or devalues or gives time a metahistorical meaning and who accords the historical moment no value in itself. Both Billy and Milton's Adam leave their "hills of foresight" armed with the knowledge that time is not as deadly as it might seem and that death's sting is not all that sharp, but the kinds of comfort they take from their knowledge are vastly different. They have to be. Adam needs the knowledge he has acquired to arm himself against the world of suffering he is about to enter. Billy, on the other hand, is leaving the Adamic world of suffering to discover timelessness.

The cosmic and mundane questions that Vonnegut and Milton seek to address in their works, then, are comparable even if their views of life and beyond differ radically, being, as they are, products of their times and belief. The motions of Milton's Adam reflect the poet's own belief in God as the ground of all goodness. By contrast, Vonnegut's Billy Pilgrim reveals a lack of faith in God and, to a large extent, a lack of confidence in humanity. The only paradise that Billy can hope to inhabit is a self-generated one where there are "no conflicts or tensions," where he can be "absolved from the guilts of war without the cost of compassion," where humankind, though "no longer the image of God, the center of the universe," is, for that very reason, no longer responsible for the horrors of history. Giannone has pointed out that the Tralfamadorians "play God, but without his merciful concern for creation"—a concern that is abundantly evidenced throughout Milton's theodicean epic. But this concern is, of course, deliberately missing from Billy's reinvented world view, replaced by a deterministic existence in which nothing needs to be explained or rectified since free will can do nothing to change conditions.

To be sure, Billy's solution does not answer the needs of all of humanity. It is too contrived, idiosyncratic, and self-serving for that; and it would be a mistake to believe that Vonnegut himself is advancing any such notion. In fact, some critics have interpreted the novel's meaning in just this way, arguing that Vonnegut reveals in *Slaughterhouse-Five* his own indifference to questions of ethical conduct and his preference for facile and fantastic moral code. Nothing can be further from the truth, however. If anything, Vonnegut's novels are a plea for ethical action, for the exercise of reason, for human will to be placed at the service of peace. Billy Pilgrim is not Kurt Vonnegut, nor is Billy the sort of person that Vonnegut is inviting his readers to emulate, though, to a limited extent, we cannot but sympathize and therefore identify with him. As I have noted elsewhere, one of Vonnegut's great strengths as a writer is his ability to force us to look at the world from dual perspectives—as, so to speak, outsiders and insiders. Like all ironic fictions, *Slaughterhouse-Five* invites the reader to look down upon the characters and events of the fiction. From a safe and superior intellectual distance, we regard Billy Pilgrim as a pathetic figure, at once weak-willed, passive, and victimized by both his own diseased mind and the brutal forces of politics. By the same token, however, Vonnegut also allows us glimpses into Billy's internal reality—his desire for peace and love, for innocence, for stability and escape from the world's madness. These glimpses are meant to appeal to our own common yearnings. Seen from that perspective, Billy Pilgrim, the Pilgrim-Everyman, is indeed all of us.

This duality of vision is what allows *Slaughterhouse-Five* to be more than the lurid and ludicrous tale of a lone madman and his obsessive behaviors. Rather, its subtext, like that of all of Vonnegut's novels, is a plea for responsible action, for change, for the pursuit of Genesis not as a lost mythic ideal but as an attainable state of innocence. And, as we will see, that plea will grow more and more pronounced in Vonnegut's more recent novels.

WILLIAM RODNEY ALLEN

Slaughterhouse-Five

Nearly a quarter of a century passed between the night Kurt Vonnegut survived the firebombing of Dresden in World War II and the publication of his fictionalized account of that event, *Slaughterhouse-Five*. As Vonnegut says, "It seemed a categorical imperative that I write about Dresden, the firebombing of Dresden, since it was the largest massacre in the history of Europe and I am a person of European extraction and I, a writer, had been present. I *had* to say something about it." But the problem was, as Vonnegut remarks in the novel itself, "There is nothing intelligent to say about a massacre." Consequently he was frustrated in his early attempts to tell the single story he felt he had to tell: "I came home in 1945, started writing about it, and wrote about it, and *wrote about it* and WROTE ABOUT IT. . . . The book is a process of twenty years of this sort of living with Dresden and the aftermath." Precisely because the story was so hard to tell, and because Vonnegut was willing to take the two decades necessary to tell it—to speak the unspeakable—*Slaughterhouse-Five* is a great novel, a masterpiece sure to remain a permanent part of American literature.

The story of Dresden was a hard one for an American to tell for a simple reason: it was designed by the Allies to kill as many German civilians as possible, and it was staggeringly successful in achieving that aim. Because the government rebuffed his attempts shortly after the war to obtain

From *Understanding Kurt Vonnegut.* © 1991 University of South Carolina.

information about the Dresden bombing, saying only that it was classified, it took Vonnegut years to realize the scale of the destruction of life on the night of February 13, 1945. What he eventually learned was that, by the most conservative estimates, 135,000 people died in the raid—far more than were killed by either of the atomic bombs the United States dropped later that year on Hiroshima and Nagasaki. Vonnegut was not killed himself in the attack by purest chance: he and a few other American POWs and their guards had available to them perhaps the only effective bomb shelter in the city, a meat locker two stories underground. They and only a handful of others survived the attack. This massive destruction of life was achieved by a technological breakthrough of sorts—the combination of two kinds of bombs that produced far greater devastation than either could have alone. As Vonnegut explained in an interview:

> They went over with high explosives first to loosen things up, and then scattered incendiaries. When the war started, incendiaries were fairly sizeable, about long as a shoebox. By the time Dresden got it, they were tiny little things. They burnt the whole damn town down. . . . A fire storm is an amazing thing. It doesn't occur in nature. It's fed by the tornadoes that occur in the midst of it and there isn't a damned thing to breathe. . . . It was a fancy thing to see, a startling thing. It was a moment of truth, too, because American civilians and ground troops didn't know American bombers were engaged in saturation bombing.

In another interview he said, "When we went into the war, we felt our Government was a respecter of life, careful about not injuring civilians and that sort of thing. Well, Dresden had no tactical value; it was a city of civilians. Yet the Allies bombed it until it burned and melted. And then they lied about it. All that was startling to us."

Yet as crucial as Vonnegut's experience at Dresden was to his life and his fictional career, he has resisted the temptation to overdramatize it, to raise it to an apotheosis of the sort Hemingway did of his wounding in World War I at the Italian front. When asked if the events at Dresden changed him, Vonnegut replied, "No. I suppose you'd think so, because that's the cliché. The importance of Dresden in my life has been considerably exaggerated because my book about it became a best seller. If the book hadn't been a best seller, it would seem like a very minor experience in my life." Dresden, then, was no road-to-Damascus–like conversion to a totally new way of thinking for Vonnegut; he was, after all, a young man convinced like most Americans of the necessity of destroying Nazism by whatever means necessary. The change came gradually, as a long process of thinking about the nature of war and writing about it, at first unsuccessfully. Finally, Vonnegut was less affected by the actual experience of Dresden than he would be by the fame that came with the enormous popularity of his book on the subject.

As James Lundquist puts it, Vonnegut's task in writing the novel was somehow to bridge "the increasing gap between the horrors of life in the twentieth century and our imaginative ability to comprehend their full actuality." Indeed, what *can* one say about the madness in our time of human beings slaughtering their fellow human beings—coldly, methodically, scientifically, in numbers heretofore inconceivable? In his book *The Great War and Modern Memory*, Paul Fussell says that World War I was such a shock to those who experienced it that the only response they found adequate to describe it in literature was a searing irony. One thinks of such literary products of the war as Wilfred Owen's "Dulce et Decorum Est," a poem contrasting the martial phrase from Cicero that it is "sweet and proper" to die for one's country with the grotesque, panic-stricken death of soldiers in a mustard gas attack. But if World War I was a shock with its machine guns, its heavy artillery, and its trench-warfare charges into no-man's land, what of the next war with its saturation bombings, its death camps, its atomic bombs? Like the post–World War I writers Vonnegut had to find a new way to convey the horror, a new form to reflect a new kind of consciousness. He used irony, to be sure, but he went further, by altering the fundamental processes of narration itself. More than a conventional reminiscence of war, *Slaughterhouse-Five* is an attempt to describe a new mode of perception that radically alters traditional conceptions of time and morality.

Put most simply, what Vonnegut says about time in the novel is that it does not necessarily "point" only in one direction, from past to future. As Lundquist observes, "The novel functions to reveal new viewpoints in somewhat the same way that the theory of relativity broke through the concepts of absolute space and time." Twenty years after the publication of *Slaughterhouse-Five*, theoretical physicists like Stephen F. Hawking are becoming more convinced that there is no reason why under some circumstances the "arrow of time" might point from future to past rather than from past to future. If such a reversal is possible, then the famous description in *Slaughterhouse-Five* of a backwards movie (in which air force planes suck up bombs into themselves from the ground and fly backwards to their bases, where soldiers unload the bombs and ship them back to the factories to be disassembled) might be more than a wistful fantasy of a peaceful world. Of course, Vonnegut is less interested in new theories in physics than he is in his characters' confrontations with a world that makes no sense in terms of their old ways of seeing it. Hence, rather than beginning his story by quoting Einstein, Vonnegut puts a particular person in a very particular situation: "Listen: Billy Pilgrim has come unstuck in time."

But that striking opening sentence comes not in chapter 1 but in chapter 2. Chapter 1 consists of Vonnegut speaking in his own voice about the difficulties of writing *Slaughterhouse-Five*. Beginning with his 1966 introduction to the reissued *Mother Night*, Vonnegut had begun to speak more openly about himself and about the autobiographical connections underlying his writing. In the opening and closing chapters of *Slaughterhouse-Five*, however, he takes that process much further. By making the autobiographical "frame" of the novel part of the novel itself (rather than setting those sections apart as a preface and an afterword) Vonnegut, as Lundquist puts it, "conceptualizes his own life the way he later does Billy's, in terms of Tralfamadorian time theory. The structure of the chapter about writing the novel consequently prefigures the structure of the novel itself." Vonnegut jumps from how he returned to Dresden in 1967 on a Guggenheim fellowship with his "old war buddy," Bernard V. O'Hare, to what it had been like to try to write about Dresden just after the war, to his first meeting after the war with O'Hare in Philadelphia, to his time teaching in the Writer's Workshop at the University of Iowa. Yet as Reed observes, "There is surprisingly little difficulty in following this seemingly disjointed narrative. The prologue [of] the first chapter, and the quick general guidelines to Billy's life in the second, provide the reader with a strong sense of direction from the outset."

Perhaps most helpful is Vonnegut's discussion in chapter 1 of his failed attempts at writing a traditional narrative about Dresden—one with an Aristotelian beginning, middle, and end:

> As a trafficker in climaxes and thrills and characterization and wonderful dialogue and suspense and confrontations, I had outlined the Dresden story many times. The best outline I ever made, or anyway the prettiest one, was on the back of a roll of wallpaper.
>
> I used my daughter's crayons, a different color for each main character. One end of the wallpaper was the beginning of the story, and the other end was the end, and then there was all that middle part, which was the middle. And the blue line met the red line and then the yellow line, and the yellow line stopped because the character represented by the yellow line was dead. And so on. The destruction of Dresden was represented by a vertical band of orange cross-hatching, and all the lines that were still alive passed through it, came out the other side.

There are many reasons why such a traditional structure did not work for the novel Vonnegut wanted to write, but the principal one is that characters' lives, like those of real people, do not themselves proceed in one direction: in reality one does as much "backward" traveling in time through memory as "forward" traveling in anticipation of the future. Thus while not identical with it, *Slaughterhouse-Five*'s narrative mode is allied with the stream-of-consciousness technique pioneered by Joyce and Faulkner, which seeks to reproduce the mind's simultaneous blending of the past through memory, the present through perception, and the future through anticipation. Vonnegut's own life, and Billy Pilgrim's, is characterized by an obsessive return to the past. Like Lot's wife in the Bible, mentioned at the end of chapter 1, Vonnegut could not help looking back, despite the danger of being turned metaphorically into a pillar of salt, into an emblem of the death that comes to those who cannot let go of the past. To get to the heart of the matter of Dresden, moreover, Vonnegut felt he had to let go of the writer's usual bag of chronological tricks—suspense and confrontations and climaxes—and proceed by a different logic toward the future of the novel form.

Thus Vonnegut gives away what would be the traditional climax of his book—the execution of Billy's friend Edgar Derby "for taking a teapot that wasn't his"—in the novel's first paragraph. Throughout the novel he intentionally deflates suspense by mentioning in advance the outcome of any conflict he creates. The readers learn early, for example, that Billy will be kidnapped and taken to the planet Tralfamadore in 1967, where he will learn of the very different ways the Tralfamadorians view the universe. He learns as well that Billy will be shot to death on February 13, 1976, by Paul Lazzaro, a paranoid sadist Billy had been captured with in the war. He even learns with Billy the ultimate fate of the universe: the Tralfamadorians will accidently blow it up while experimenting with a new type of rocket fuel. Thus, rather than being like a straight line, the narrative chronology of *Slaughterhouse-Five* is more like an ascending, widening spiral that circles over the same territory yet does so from an ever higher and wider perspective. Finally, like most science fiction writers, Vonnegut hopes to push the reader's perceptual horizon as far as he can toward infinity—toward the union of all time and all space. There mystery remains, even though suspense disappears, since suspense is a function of a lack of knowledge at a single point in time and space.

Paradoxically, in creating this cosmic, nonlinear narrative Vonnegut uses fragments of all sorts of traditional narrative forms, much as a bird might use twigs, bits of string, and its own feathers to construct a nest, something very different than the sum of its parts. As Richard Giannone observes, "Graffiti, war memos, anecdotes, jokes, songs—light operatic and liturgical—raw statistics, assorted tableaux, flash before the reader's eye." The most important linear narrative underlying all of these is the Judeo-Christian Bible, which is itself a central motif in *Slaughterhouse-Five*. There time proceeds from the creation to man's fall to the birth, crucifixion, and resurrection of Christ to the end of time with the Second Coming. Giannone suggests that the Gospels were "an amalgamation of language forms that were available to early Christians to spread their good tidings, rather than a fixed ideal shape sent down out of the blue. . . . [Yet] the old forms were inadequate to convey the momentous news, so primitive Christians made their own." Thus Vonnegut tries in *Slaughterhouse-Five* to do what the Gospel writers attempted to do in their time: construct a new form out of the fragments of old forms.

That Vonnegut was conscious of doing so—that he found the Christian, linear vision of time no longer adequate—is apparent by his remarks in the novel on a book by Kilgore Trout called *The Gospel from Outer Space*. According to Trout, the traditional Gospels are flawed because they seem to suggest that the moral lesson one should learn from Jesus' crucifixion is: *"Before you kill somebody, make absolutely sure he isn't well connected."* In Trout's revised version of the story, rather than being the Son of God, "Jesus really *was* a nobody, and a pain in the neck to a lot of people with better connections than he had. He still got to say all the lovely and puzzling things he said in the other Gospels." Yet when this nobody is crucified, the heavens open up with thunder and lightning, and God announces that he *"will punish horribly anybody who torments a bum who has no connections."* In the course of the novel it becomes clear that the weak, hapless, clownishly dressed Billy Pilgrim is precisely this "bum who has no connections"—that he is in effect a sort of new Christ. Such observations as the fact that Billy lay "self-crucified" on a brace in his German POW boxcar, or that Billy "resembled the Christ of the carol" that Vonnegut takes as the novel's epigraph ("The cattle are lowing, / The baby awakes. / But the little Lord Jesus / No crying he makes.") make clear that this identification of Billy as a Christ-figure is Vonnegut's conscious intention.

Like Christ, Billy brings a new message to the world, although it is a very different one from his predecessor's. And like Jesus he is an innocent who accepts his death, at the hands of an enemy who reviles and misunderstands him, as an opportunity to teach mankind the proper response to mortality. Both Billy and Jesus teach that one should face death calmly, because death is not the end. In the Christian vision the self after death proceeds forward in time eternally, either in heaven or hell; for Billy, however, "after" death the soul proceeds backward in time, back into life. As Billy learns from the Tralfamadorians,

> When a person dies he only *appears* to die. He is still very much alive in the past, so it is very silly for people to cry at this funeral.

All moments, past, present, and future, always have existed, always will exist. The Tralfamadorians can look at all the different moments just the way we can look at a stretch of the Rocky Mountains, for instance. They can see how permanent all the moments are, and they can look at any moment that interests them. It is just an illusion we have here on Earth that one moment follows another one, like beads on a string, and that once a moment is gone it is gone forever.

Thus Billy, the new Christ, preaches that human beings do have eternal life— even if there is no life after death.

The literary consequence of the Tralfamadorian conception of time is the Tralfamadorian novel, which consists of "brief clumps of symbols read simultaneously." As the Tralfamadorians tell Billy, these symbols, or messages, when seen all at once "produce an image of life that is beautiful and surprising and deep. There is no beginning, no middle, no end, no suspense, no moral, no causes, no effects." *Slaughterhouse-Five* is of course itself an attempt to write this sort of book, as Vonnegut announces in his subtitle: "This is a novel somewhat in the telegraphic schizophrenic manner of tales of the planet Tralfamadore." While human beings cannot read all the passages of the book simultaneously, its short length, its scrambled chronology, its deft juxtapositionings of different times to make thematic points, and its intricate patterns of imagery all combine to give the reader something of that effect. Once he finishes the novel—after a few hours, perhaps in one sitting—the reader can visualize all of Billy's moments stretched out before him like the Rocky Mountains; further, he can see the author's life in the same way, all the way from World War II to the assassination of Robert Kennedy in 1968, when Vonnegut was composing the last pages of *Slaughterhouse-Five*.

Yet while the novel boldly attempts to do away with traditional chronological narration on one level, it still gives the reader a story that builds toward the bombing of Dresden, which is recounted in greatest detail late in the book. Rather than being a traditional novel or a purely experimental, "Tralfamadorian" novel, *Slaughterhouse-Five* is more like one superimposed on the other. One can easily follow the traditional *Bildungsroman* of Billy's life. Born in 1922, like his creator, he endured a childhood marked by intense fears—of drowning when his father subjected him to the "sink or swim method," of falling into the Grand Canyon on a family trip, of the total darkness when the guides extinguished the lights in Carlsbad Caverns. These early images have great relevance for Billy's fear and ineptitude in the war and afterward. His refusal to try to swim and consequent passive sinking to the bottom of the pool is a symbolic wish to return to the safety of the womb. Billy falls constantly in the novel—into ditches, from boxcars, from the sky in a plane crash—despite his intense fear of falling epitomized by his Grand Canyon experience. Finally, the darkness in Carlsbad Caverns prefigures that in the meat locker two stories underground in Dresden—the most important symbolic womb into which Billy retreats for safety. One of the many ironies of the book is that such a passive person should be one of the few to survive the destruction of the city. As Vonnegut says simply of his hero, "He was unenthusiastic about living."

After this shaky childhood Billy attends college for only a few weeks before going off to war as an unarmed chaplain's assistant. In no time he is captured, along with a hapless tank gunner named Roland Weary, in the Battle of the Bulge, the last great German counteroffensive of the war. Freezing in inadequate clothing, hungry, frightened out of his wits, Billy becomes "unstuck in time" for the first time, finding himself living moments out of his past or his future. Weary dies in transit to the POW camp of gangrene of the feet, which he had claimed was caused when the time-tripping Billy abstractedly stepped on him. Before he dies, Weary tells his story to Paul Lazzaro, who vows to avenge Weary's death by tracking Billy down after the war and killing him. Lazzaro is an emblem of the fact that a soldier can never really escape his war experiences—that they will always "track him down" even years later. In the POW camp the dispirited group of Americans is greeted by some hale and hearty Englishmen who have been there most of the war, growing healthy on good Red Cross food (sent by mistake in excessive amounts), exercise, and English optimism. They are the opposite of Billy, the fatalistic, disheveled weakling who simply drifts from one disaster to the next in helpless resignation. After a falling out with the Englishmen over personal hygiene and philosophical attitudes, the Americans are sent to Dresden, a supposedly "open" city, where they soon have their rendezvous with the most significant day in the city's history, February 13, 1945.

After the war Billy does far better than one would expect, since he becomes an optometrist, marries the boss's daughter, and is soon driving a Cadillac, living in an all-electric home, and pulling in over $60,000 a year. But the thematic reason Vonnegut makes Billy so successful is perhaps more important than the slight problem of verisimilitude: Vonnegut wants to show that all Billy's material comforts—his magic fingers bed, the expensive jewelry he gives Valencia, his wife, his fancy car (which will be the cause of his wife's death)—can do nothing to smooth over the pain of what he has experienced. Shortly after the war Billy had checked himself into a mental hospital, where he received shock treatments for depression. Today his problem would be called posttraumatic stress syndrome. Late in the novel, as he feels agony while listening to a barbershop quartet sing "That Old Gang of Mine" at a party celebrating his wedding anniversary, Billy realizes that "he had a great big secret somewhere inside," even though "he could not imagine what it was." His secret is of course the awareness of the horrors of war and the certainty of death—an awareness the frantic materialism of postwar America was desperately trying to cover up.

The cracks in the American dream show through Billy's apparently successful postwar life. Valencia is a parody of consumerism, since she constantly consumes candy bars while making empty promises to lose weight in order to please Billy sexually. Billy's son appears to be headed for jail as a teen-ager before he joins the Green Berets and goes off to fight in Vietnam. On his way to the office Billy stops at a traffic light in a burned-out ghetto area and drives away when a black man tries to talk with him. Vonnegut was obviously responding to the incredible social tensions of the late 1960s, which saw the burning of major portions of several American cities in race riots, the assassinations of John F. Kennedy, Martin Luther King, Jr., and Robert Kennedy, and the seemingly endless acceleration of the war in Vietnam. A major reason *Slaughterhouse-Five* had the enormous impact it did was because it was published at the height of the conflict in Vietnam, and so delivered its antiwar message to a most receptive audience. In a book of powerful passages, there is no more powerful one than this at the end of the novel, in Vonnegut's autobiographical chapter 10: "Robert Kennedy, whose summer home is eight miles from the home I live in all year round, was shot two nights ago. He died last night." One of Robert Kennedy's promises in his presidential campaign was to stop the war, and when he died that hope seemed to die with him. For Vonnegut, and for Billy, it must have seemed that Dresden was happening all over again in Vietnam.

In 1967, on the night of his daughter's wedding, Billy is picked up by a flying saucer and taken in a time warp to Tralfamadore, where he is displayed in a sort of Tralfamadorian zoo by his abductors. Since Billy had not been very happy on earth, he finds that during his stay of several years (in terms of Tralfamadorian time, not Earth time) he is "about as happy as I was on Earth." His happiness is increased when the Tralfamadorians kidnap a sexy movie actress, Montana Wildhack, and bring her to the zoo as Billy's "mate." So while Billy enjoys sexual bliss for the first time with the willing Ms. Wildhack, he gets instruction from the Tralfamadorians on the true nature of the universe. Billy and Montana appear as a sort of new Adam and Eve, who live in the confines of a perfect world, until Billy eats from the tree of knowledge, in effect, by learning the true nature of time and the place of conscious beings in the universe. He is expelled from his symbolic garden when the Tralfamadorians (for unexplained reasons) send him back to Earth. An enlightened Billy then begins his mission of preaching his new gospel to his fellowmen—who are understandably skeptical about his claims.

Vonnegut leaves room for the idea that Billy's trip to Tralfamadore is all in Billy's mind. This sort of "escape hatch" from fantasy into realism is characteristic of the sci-fi genre: in *A Connecticut Yankee in King Author's Court* Twain has his hero receive a blow on the head and probably dream the novel's events. In *Slaughterhouse-Five* Billy had been in a mental hospital and received shock treatments. During his stay there he had met Eliot Rosewater, who makes a cameo appearance from Vonnegut's previous novel in order to introduce Billy to the sci-fi works of Kilgore Trout. One of the novels Billy reads, *The Big Board*, concerns an Earth couple kidnapped by aliens and displayed on their planet in a zoo. An event in 1968, moreover, suggests a physical explanation for the Tralfamadorian episodes: Billy survives a plane crash on the way to an optometrists' convention that kills everyone else and leaves him with a serious head injury. In chapter 1 of the novel Vonnegut mentions the French writer Céline, who had received a head wound fighting in World War I, and who had thereafter heard voices and had written his death-obsessed novels during his sleepless nights. Like Billy, Céline too was obsessed with time: Billy's Tralfamadore experience may be seen as the equivalent of Céline's—and Vonnegut's—attempts to deal with the problem of mortality through writing fiction. As Vonnegut observes of Rosewater and Billy, "They had both found life meaningless, partly because of what they had seen in war. . . . So they were trying to re-invent themselves and their universe. Science fiction was a big help."

Billy's trip to Tralfamadore, then, finally begins to look more like a metaphor than a literal description of events. His space travel is simply a way for Vonnegut to describe the growth of his own imagination out of the Christian, linear vision of time to the cosmic perspective of time as the fourth dimension. This is not to say, however, that Vonnegut offers the Tralfamadorian *attitudes* toward that vision as final truth. Tralfamadorians— "real" or imagined—are not human beings, so that their attitude of absolute indifference toward the terrors of the universe—even to the ultimate terror of its annihilation—could never work for humans. If *Slaughterhouse-Five* is a combination of the traditional narrative and the Tralfamadorian novel, it is also a synthesis of Christian and Tralfamadorian morals: the reader is not so much urged to choose the latter over the former as to superimpose the two. When Billy passionately implores the Tralfamadorians to tell him how they live in peace, so that he can return to give that knowledge to Earth, his hosts reply that war and peace come and go at random on Tralfamadore as they do everywhere else. Their response to any frustration on Billy's part—to his profoundly human need to know why—is simply that "there is no *why*." When

Billy wonders why the universe must blow up, they respond that "the moment is structured that way." The Tralfamadorians claim that "only on Earth is there any talk of free will." Such profound indifference could never suffice for human beings, nor does Vonnegut imply that it should.

Slaughterhouse-Five is built on the paradox that it appears to offer acceptance and even indifference as responses to the horrors of the twentieth century, when in fact it is a moving lament over those horrors—a piercing wail of grief over the millions of dead in World War II. Emblematic of this paradox is a short phrase from the novel that has become probably the best-known and most often repeated by his readers of any in Vonnegut's work: "So it goes." In *Palm Sunday* Vonnegut explains that the phrase was his response to his reading of Céline's *Journey to the End of Night*: "It was a clumsy way of saying what Céline managed to imply . . . in everything he wrote, in effect: 'Death and suffering can't matter nearly as much as I think they do. Since they are so common, my taking them so seriously must mean that I am insane.'" Every time someone dies in the novel—from Wild Bob to Valencia to Billy Pilgrim himself to Robert Kennedy—Vonnegut repeats "So it goes." Once this pattern is established, Vonnegut has fun with it, as when he has Billy pick up a bottle of flat champagne after his daughter's wedding: "The champagne was dead. So it goes." Thus the phrase finally embodies all the essential attitudes toward death in the novel—acceptance, sorrow, humor, outrage. If at times "So it goes" reads like a resigned "Let it be," it more often comes through as the reverse: "Let it be *different*—let all these dead live!" So Vonnegut does let them live, in effect, by positing the Tralfamadorian idea that they are always alive in their pasts.

Despite its mask of Tralfamadorian indifference *Slaughterhouse-Five* conveys at times an almost childlike sense of shock that the world is such a violent place. Children form an important motif in the book, which is subtitled "The Children's Crusade." Vonnegut had chosen that ironic phrase as a way to reassure Mary O'Hare, Bernard's wife, that he was not going to portray war as a glamorous affair fought by "Frank Sinatra and John Wayne or some of those other glamorous war-loving, dirty old men." When the British POWs, after several years in captivity, see Billy and the other recently captured Americans, they confess that "we had forgotten that wars were fought by babies." Before recounting the bombing of Dresden, Billy and his young German guard see a group of adolescent girls taking a shower. They are "utterly beautiful." Yet when the bombs begin to fall, Vonnegut records that "the girls that Billy had seen naked were all being killed. . . . So it goes."

But *Slaughterhouse-Five* does not stop with the pathos of innocent children being killed. It refuses to be a self-satisfied antiwar book like, say, *Johnny Got His Gun*. While conveying a sense of outrage, horror, regret, and even despair over the insanity of war, Vonnegut does not think that stopping war is a realistic possibility or that, if it were, this would end the pain of the human condition. In chapter 1, when talking about his Dresden project to a movie producer, Vonnegut had gotten the response, "'Why don't you write an anti-*glacier* book instead?' What he meant, of course, was that there would always be wars, that they were as easy to stop as glaciers. I believe that, too." Even more significant is Vonnegut's admission that "if wars didn't keep coming like glaciers, there would still be plain old death." Finally, while Vonnegut accepts war and death as inevitable, he refuses to endorse the sentimentalized, childlike attitude of acceptance of the inevitable epitomized in the prayer hanging on Billy's office wall and inside a locket on a chain hanging around Montana Wildhack's neck: "God grant me the serenity to accept the things I cannot change, courage to change the things I can, and wisdom always to tell the difference." As Vonnegut observes, "Among the things Billy Pilgrim could not change were the past, the present, and the future." Dresden has happened, is happening, and will always happen.

Yet if the war is always going on, it is always ending, too. Life comes out of death, as surely as Billy survives the bombing of Dresden in a slaughterhouse. In chapter 1 Vonnegut describes the end of the war, when thousands of POWs of all nationalities were gathered in a beetfield by the Elbe River. This moment of liberation of the soldiers of all countries would grow for twenty years in Vonnegut's mind until it became the central image in *Bluebeard*, his most recent novel. The last sound in *Slaughterhouse-Five* is not that of bombs falling, but of a bird chirping just after the war: "*Poo-tee-weet?*" By making the chirp a question Vonnegut seems to ask all the survivors of the war, "Despite everything, would you like to try again?"

Reed speaks for most critics of Vonnegut's writing when he says, that "*Slaughterhouse-Five* remains a remarkably successful novel . . . [that] neither falters from, nor sensationalizes the horrors it depicts, and tenaciously avoids pedantic or moralistic commentary; no small achievement given the subject matter and the author's personal closeness to it." Vonnegut was indeed close to the events of *Slaughterhouse-Five*, but it took him nearly a quarter of a century to get far enough away from them in time to have the proper perspective. The authority of that perspective perhaps most forcefully rings through the simple phrase Billy utters about Dresden near the novel's end: lying in his hospital bed after his plane crash, listening to Bertrand Rumfoord belittle the "bleeding hearts" who would mourn the loss of innocent life in the Allied firebombings, Billy responds: "I was there." Finally, *Slaughterhouse-Five* gains its power not as an act of moralizing, but of witness.

JEROME KLINKOWITZ

Emerging from Anonymity

At the beginning of 1969 Kurt Vonnegut was forty-six years old and the author of five novels, two short-story collections, forty-six separately published short stories (in magazines as familiar as *Collier's* and the *Saturday Evening Post*), and twenty feature essays and reviews. However, he was almost totally unknown—unknown in public terms, that is. With his more than half a million words in print, editors knew him—but as a professional pigeonholed as doing science fiction or selling to the slicks rather than as a major voice in American culture. True, much of his production was undertaken, by necessity, in commercial fashion. Rejected stories with a technical theme were shuttled off to the nickel-a-word venues of *Argosy* and *Worlds of If;* when the family magazine markets dried up, he found he could make the same money by outlining paperback originals, which is how some of his most important novels were conceived; and to support himself and his large family by his writing he undertook review assignments on far from literary topics. But compared to other major writers at similar stages in their careers, Kurt Vonnegut at midpoint was laboring in virtual obscurity, writing fiction and fact alike that were not having any public impact beyond a moment's entertainment and another month's expenses met.

Beginning in March of 1969, all that changed. With the publication of his sixth novel, *Slaughterhouse-Five*, Vonnegut found himself in unlikely

From *Vonnegut in Fact: The Public Spokesmanship of Personal Fiction.* © 1998 University of South Carolina.

107

places: as the lead item in the most prominent national book reviews and as a major presence on the best-seller lists of these same newspapers and journals. Quality alone is rarely the distinguishing factor in such attention. In Vonnegut's case, subsequent scholarship has shown that *Cat's Cradle* and *Mother Night* are as significant achievements as *Slaughterhouse-Five*, yet the former never outsold its first printing of six thousand copies and received just a few passing reviews, while the latter's debut as a paperback original meant no media coverage at all, a fate shared with *The Sirens of Titan*, another work now considered central to the Vonnegut canon. Rather, as any publicist will testify, getting reviewed by major critics on the front pages of book sections is a privilege mostly reserved for the country's best-known authors. Getting there as an unknown is a rare achievement indeed, the reasons for which merit close study.

A correlation exists between the first two major reviews of *Slaughterhouse-Five*: each was written by a critic who had heard Vonnegut speak to audiences, and who had been, moreover, deeply impressed by the personal voice in the author's fictive statement. Not that public speaking was Kurt Vonnegut's chosen profession; rather, his talk at Notre Dame University's Literary Festival (as heard by Granville Hicks) and his two-year lectureship at the University of Iowa (where Robert Scholes was a colleague) were stopgap measures to generate some income after his customary publishing markets had either closed (as in the case of *Collier's* and the *Post*) or ceased to respond. Those who have met him know he is a quiet person much protective of his privacy; for him, public speaking is a nervous chore. More than once he has observed of a lecture that instead of courting laughs and easy applause he should be at home doing his real work, writing novels. But with the relative failure of his fifth novel, *God Bless You, Mr. Rosewater*, to make much headway in 1965, novel writing was no longer an option, and so Vonnegut accepted a teaching position at the University of Iowa Writers' Workshop and booked speeches at literary festivals and library dedications around the country as ways of matching the modest income his short stories and paperback originals had generated before.

This was what was known to Granville Hicks in 1969, when the venerable old critic (who had made his initial mark as a commentator on socially radical literature of the Great Depression era) was faced with introducing an unknown author to his readers in the *Saturday Review*. The new novel itself, *Slaughterhouse-Five*, was an equally difficult topic, for its innovative format was worlds away from the realistic, sociologically based fiction Hicks had championed for nearly half a century. Therefore the critic began discussing what he *did* know: that the year before he and a student audience at Notre Dame had heard Kurt Vonnegut deliver "as funny a lecture as I had ever listened to." Given what Vonnegut then had in print—a few paperback editions gaudily dressed as space opera—his audience might have expected the wooly ruminations of a science fiction writer. But after hearing him speak, no one present could mistake Kurt Vonnegut for a Harlan Ellison, Isaac Asimov, or even for his affectionately drawn portrait of the perennially misunderstood SF hack, Kilgore Trout. "What he really is," Hicks announced, "is a sardonic humorist and satirist in the vein of Mark Twain and Jonathan Swift." Twain and Swift, of course, are remarkable as two of the English language's great public writers, spokesmen who addressed the crucial issues of their day in the most direct manner and in the most personably appropriate voice. There was much of that same quality in Vonnegut, Hicks learned in the audience that night, and he encountered it again in the pages of *Slaughterhouse-Five*, in which the same real-life person speaks directly to the reader in chapters 1 and 10.

Science Fiction, Hicks realized, was at least a tangential concern in the author's earlier work: *Player Piano, Cat's Cradle,* and *God Bless You, Mr. Rosewater* had made great fun of the worship of science and technology; misfunctions of both were responsible for catastrophes of plot and hilarities of incident, not to mention a dim overview of human strivings toward a mechanical ideal. But *Slaughterhouse-Five* was more autobiographically revealing. "Now we can see," Hicks revealed, "that his quarrel with contemporary society began with his experiences in World War II, about which he has at last managed to write a book." From here Hicks went directly to Vonnegut's most personal statement to the reader, his confession that "I would hate to tell you what this lousy little book cost me in money and anxiety and time." From Vonnegut's admission of problems in writing his book, Hicks proceeds to the second key factor: that "All this happened, more or less," another personal confession that violates even more seriously the convention that an author must maintain a certain distance from his or her work. It is this personal relationship that makes the novel interesting. It is, in fact, the only thing the book truly has, since its purported subject, the firebombing of Dresden late in World War II, is something "Vonnegut never does get around to describing." What matters is that "Like Mark Twain, Vonnegut feels sadness as well as indignation when he looks at the damned human race," and in *Slaughterhouse-Five* he has found a vehicle for expressing that very personal view. "There is nothing intelligent to say about a massacre," the author tells his publisher; yet as Granville Hicks reads what Vonnegut offers in place of such conclusive statements, "I could hear Vonnegut's mild voice, see his dead pan as he told a ludicrous story, and gasp as I grasped the terrifying implications of some calm remark." The reaction, then, is to a public spokesman: one who not only addresses himself to a topic of great common interest, but who fashions his own reaction as an expression of what he feels should be the socially and culturally responsible view.

Even more instrumental in presenting Kurt Vonnegut's new novel to the public was Robert Scholes's front-page coverage in the *New York Times Book Review*. Personal articulation of a common cause was the first thing Scholes pointed out—"Kurt Vonnegut speaks with the voice of the 'silent generation,' and his quiet words explain the quiescence of his contemporaries"—and, like Granville Hicks, the reviewer was familiar with the author, having been his colleague at the University of Iowa as recently as the 1965–1967 academic years. To Scholes, Vonnegut's message was a simple one, its testimony an act of witness. The novel's speaking voice is plain and simple, suiting its message that one had best be kind and unhurtful because "Death is coming for all of us anyway, and it is better to be Lot's wife looking back through salty eyes than the Deity that destroyed those cities of the plain in order to save them."

Because he sees himself in his act of witnessing as Lot's wife, the author of *Slaughterhouse-Five* judges himself a failure. Robert Scholes thinks not, but feels that "Serious critics have shown some reluctance to acknowledge that Vonnegut is among the best writers of his generation" because he is "too funny and too intelligent for many, who confuse muddled earnestness with profundity." Yet it is his plain and honest approach, which cuts through the obscuring technicalities of morals and philosophies, that allows "the cruelest deeds" to be "done in the best causes," while writers whose language and approach are immensely more sophisticated find it impossible to convince their readers that "our problems are not in our institutions but ourselves."

Accompanying Robert Scholes's review was a background piece on Vonnegut himself by another former Iowa colleague, C. D. B. Bryan. Like Scholes, Bryan made much of the author's personal qualities, especially his "quiet, humorous, well-mannered and rational protests against man's inhumanity to man" as forming "an articulate bridge across the generation gap." Bryan reinforced this personal sense by crowding his piece with intimacies, including references to Vonnegut struggling to support his family by selling what he could to the commercial magazines and reportedly earning "what I would have made in charge of the cafeteria at a pretty good junior-high school," another folksy comment intended to make the reader feel as familiar and comfortable with the man as Bryan did.

Getting page 1 of the *New York Times Book Review* is no small accomplishment; having page 2 devoted to a personality piece is even more impressive, prompting one to ask why a generally unknown author such as Kurt Vonnegut would receive such treatment by the nation's leading review medium. One reason was the author's own persistence in making those commercial sales that kept his family supported by at least middle-class standards. One of the publications for which Vonnegut undertook relatively servile duties was the *Times Book Review* itself, reporting not a fancy best-seller or important intellectual work but rather one of the greatest challenges to a reviewer's imagination possible, *The Random House Dictionary*. What does one say about a dictionary, Vonnegut might have asked himself. In fact, his response is generated by a series of questions he asks himself as he pages through the volume's front matter and ponders what linguists argue about when debating each other's standards for inclusion or exclusion. "Prescriptive, as nearly as I could tell, was like an honest cop, and descriptive was like a boozed-up war buddy from Mobile, Ala."—such was his way of putting the editors' theoretics into terms simple and familiar enough for himself and his readers. To emphasize the shared nature of this discovery, Vonnegut reported how it emerged from conversations with two of his coworkers at Iowa, Bob Scholes and Richard Yates. But rather than sounding academic, Vonnegut's quest seemed no more complicated than simply pondering the problem, asking the guys at work about it, and then presenting his conclusion in as clear and simple and personally meaningful a way as possible.

"I find that I trust my own writing most, and others seem to trust it most, too," Vonnegut recalled several years later, "when I sound most like a person from Indianapolis, which is what I am." Such is the persona he used in the dictionary review and in most other essays he was writing at the time. One, "Science Fiction," also appeared in the *Times Book Review* and was reprinted by its editor in a volume of especially convincing personal statements. Here Vonnegut made sense of SF enthusiasts' mania to include everyone from Kafka to Tolstoy as a science fiction writer by remarking that "It is as though I were to claim that everybody of note belonged fundamentally to Delta Upsilon, my own lodge, incidentally, whether he knew it or not. Kafka would have been a desperately unhappy D.U." As in the dictionary piece, Vonnegut ranges far (by mentioning Kafka and Tolstoy as SFers), brings things back in (by talking of his own fraternity), and then makes his point by unexpectedly uniting the two (Kafka making a wretched brother of Delta Upsilon). Like the approaches of other great public speakers in the American vernacular vein—Abraham Lincoln, Mark Twain, and Will Rogers—Kurt Vonnegut makes his point by shaping his public message in the most personally familiar terms.

That Vonnegut's public spokesmanship had an infectiously personal quality to it extends to his circumstances of publication, even as those circumstances, in the case of his breakthrough book, *Slaughterhouse-Five*, encompass all that business with his friends in Iowa City and folksy appearances in the front pages of the *New York Times Book Review*. The novel itself begins with the author's own commentary on how he came to write the book, including not just its struggles of composition but the role of publisher Seymour Lawrence in bringing it to press. For his part, Lawrence revealed that what caught his attention and prompted him to buy this unknown author's next three books sight unseen was *The Random House Dictionary* review—and not just because it was brightly and amusingly written, but because it had some of its fun at the expense of Random House's Bennett Cerf, for whom Lawrence had once been a rather exasperated vice president.

The circle becomes complete when Vonnegut delivers the typescript of *Slaughterhouse-Five*, in which an actual occurrence in the book's production becomes a moment in the reader's experience of that same text. But what lies within the larger sweep of this circle, this arc of experience that stretches from an Indiana childhood through wartime service and a writer's career on the East Coast all the way back to a temporary teaching post in the Midwest where not just *Slaughterhouse-Five* but also those essays on science fiction and *The Random House Dictionary* were conceived? Before reaching the best-seller list (for the first time in his life) in Spring 1969, Kurt Vonnegut left abundant evidence of where he was heading: five novels plus all those short stories, essays, and reviews provide much for the reader to consider. But just as it was the supposedly mundane occasion of a dictionary review that brought him to the attention of Seymour Lawrence and includes so many clues to the nature of his literary genius, so does a surviving lecture from these years indicate what it was in his speaking style that impressed Granville Hicks and actually forecast the structural mode of *Slaughterhouse-Five*.

On November 21, 1967, Vonnegut appeared at Ohio State University to deliver a talk entitled "Address: To Celebrate the Accession of The Two Millionth Volume in the Collections of the Libraries of The Ohio State University." Later on, there would be many such speeches, all of them getting major media attention—on June 29, 1970, in the wake of his bestsellerdom and campus fame (during days of massive campus unrest), his commencement speech at Bennington College was reported as the lead item in *Time* magazine. But in 1967 Kurt Vonnegut was yet to be discovered, and was in fact often misunderstood—in this case by the ceremony's organizer, Professor Matthew J. Bruccoli, who was following William F. Buckley's lead at *National Review* (where Vonnegut's short story "Harrison Bergeron" was reprinted on November 16, 1965) in assuming that the author was an outspoken political conservative.

Kurt Vonnegut, of course, was and is anything but a right-wing activist, and at Columbus one finds him taking great delight in confounding expectations. He begins, just as he would in speeches after he had become famous, by warning listeners not to expect a coherent, conventionally delivered lecture. He explains that this is because he has found out there is a world of difference between sticking to a written text and interacting with a live audience. Therefore, he cautions, his audience should be ready for anything and everything, his lecture notes being just one of several texts to be flipped through and referred to in the manner of comedian Mort Sahl paging through a daily newspaper and improvising comments at random. This contrast between the formality of presenting a university lecture and the casualness of Vonnegut's approach suggests another dichotomy, one that becomes both the theme and structure of his address: the irony of having him, a college drop-out, speaking at such an august academic occasion in honor of the library acquiring its two millionth book.

It was World War II that took Kurt Vonnegut out of college, but the speaker prefers to show himself as a fugitive from the rules of formal education. Instead, he says, he wound up having to educate himself. This meant that he did his browsing for books in bus stations instead of university libraries, something that gets him his first big laugh: that it would be more appropriate, as he suggests, for him to be dedicating a new Greyhound terminal today. On such newsstands he discovered what the times had branded as tawdry fare: gaudily packaged paperbacks by D. H. Lawrence and Henry Miller, respectable editions of which continued to be banned until the Supreme Court decisions just the year before. This fascination with "dirty books" will make several appearances and is an early indication of how what the author introduces as an offhand joke seemingly tangential to the topic will become absolutely central to his enlightening argument and surprising yet convincing conclusion.

The first legacy of such an apparently shabby self-education, however, is the irony of this self-styled college dropout becoming a professor in the University of Iowa's postgraduate creative writing program, something he had been for the past two years. How did this person without so much as an undergraduate degree manage to teach master's and doctoral level students? His hope was to follow a friend's advice and not tell the class everything he knew in the first hour. An hour proved not to be the problem—after three minutes, Vonnegut explains, he was out of material. What that material was he now repeats at Ohio State, giving a quick chalk talk on the nature of storytelling derived from his anthropology thesis on the fluctuation between good and evil in simple tales—a thesis that had been rejected by the University of Chicago after the war, preserving his degreeless status.

The trick is to draw two axes and between the vertical of "good fortune/bad fortune" and the horizontal of the hero or heroine's progress to map the rise and fall in conditions. The result is comically reductive: that narratives as simple as "Cinderella" and as complex as Kafka's "The Metamorphosis" work essentially the same: that is, by measuring the protagonist's experiences in trying to distinguish the good news from the bad news. The moral is a simple one but effective in reflecting back on the speaker's situation—not just that high and low literature share the same structures, but that such patterns can be explained by a dropout chemistry major who had studied anthropology on the G.I. Bill.

As Vonnegut would refine this speech in future years, the nature of fluctuations in narratives would assume a critical dimension: that while the greatest tales, such as Shakespeare's *Hamlet*, have a relatively flat development in common with primitive stories, it is the sensationalistic crowd pleasers that take their readership on roller-coaster rides of almost hysteric highs and lows. This will be the lesson he himself learns in writing *Slaughterhouse-Five*, as Mary O'Hare cautions in the novel's first chapter: that he must resist the temptation, encouraged by Hollywood, to dress up his story in false heroics with roles tailored more for famous actors than for the haplessly common men like Kurt Vonnegut and her husband.

At Ohio State vulgar literature consisted of "Cinderella" and bus-trip abridgments of banned novels. While on the subject of vulgarity, the author pulls another of his Mort Sahl tricks, reaching for a copy of *Cosmopolitan* and citing a report that says novelists, dirty or otherwise, make lousy lovers. This draws more laughs, but Vonnegut turns them to a serious point: that these supposedly dirty books do not sell like hotcakes or sell very well at all. He names *The Rosy Crucifixion* by Henry Miller as the most sex-packed novel he knows, and then confirms that its sales are poor. What sells is not sex itself but sex stories about famous people, preferably of the gossip column variety. And even here the motive is less for stimulation than for group membership, to read what everyone else is reading and thus be able to share in conversations. In the novel he would begin soon afterward, *Breakfast of Champions*, Vonnegut would brand ideas themselves as mere badges of friendship, their conceptual content being secondary to their function as signs of human commerce, what he calls in this speech "a cheap way of saying hello."

But still there is the titillation at the idea of sex in literature, and his listeners' own awareness of that fact gets him his biggest laugh so far. "Two million!" Vonnegut marvels, crediting the number of books the Ohio State University Libraries house. "I wonder how many of them are dirty?" Before they can recover he shares another thought: "Which is the dirtiest?" Obviously meant as a joke, this question is impossible to answer—it is not meant to be answered, and knowing that they are absolved of such responsibility allows the audience to laugh along in relief. But then he turns the tables and gives them some answers, valuable in their specificity even as their checklist fashion underscores the speaker's confidence. Which is the greatest of those two million books? *Ulysses*. The noblest: *The Brothers Karamazov*. The most effective? *The Catcher in the Rye*. The most humane? *The Tenants of Moonbloom*. The most important? As Vonnegut would say in the first chapter of *Slaughterhouse-Five* in less than two years, *Death on the Installment Plan*, an important book which just now was teaching him how to handle the unspeakable nature of death—a problem that had kept his Dresden book unwritten for so long. But he had found Céline's novel without finishing college, just as he had learned similar lessons from Joyce, Dostoyevsky, Salinger, and the others. His own experience had been something like James Thurber's, who had dropped out of this very university in order to spend time reading books he cared about. Which leads to one last question: who had won the lottery, as it were, by writing the two millionth book to be acquired? Could it have been Thurber himself?

Whoever it was, it almost surely was not Kurt Vonnegut. For at this moment in his career it would have been easier to find copies of his novels at the Columbus Greyhound Terminal than at the Ohio State University Library. But maybe that was not so bad after all. As taught in college, reading great literature was turned into a version of hell week lasting all semester long, novel after massive novel being plowed through on a weekly basis until students were bleary-eyed and professors were drained of enthusiasm and ideas. What matters is his own engagement with literature, in bus stations and elsewhere—an engagement that he replicates and shares with his listeners here today.

So much of *Slaughterhouse-Five*'s method can be found in this Ohio State address: the author's introductory acknowledgment of his own insufficiency, based on the impossible nature of his assignment; the apparent digressions into seemingly unrelated subjects, only to bring those subtopics back into a mainstream argument all the stronger for its elements of surprise; his humor at the expense of himself; and yet the triumph of that self as a measure of wisdom and integrity. Just as the contradictory nature of having to say something about an unspeakable event—a massacre—generates the true subject of *Slaughterhouse-Five*, the struggle of its making, so does Kurt Vonnegut seize upon the specific problems of presenting an address on a library accession of its two millionth volume to make salient points about what that accomplishment really means. In both cases, the mode of public address is used to make his commentary possible. Indeed, because more literary approaches have proven not to work, Vonnegut must speak to his audience and readership directly—personally, and yet wearing the mantle of an otherwise unspeakable experience in a way that makes his achievement a shared occasion.

What public spokesmanship Kurt Vonnegut engaged in before the mid-1960s related more to his personal circumstances than to the profession of authorship. Yet each example relates to how public fact would become a shaping element in the way he crafted and presented his personal fictions. In the commentaries on his childhood that can be found within his works, two formative elements emerge: his pride in being instructed in old-fashioned American civics, where citizenly resourcefulness and accountability were taught not just as ideals but as practical realities, and the role that classic radio and film comedians such as Jack Benny, Fred Allen, and Laurel & Hardy played in relieving some of the personal dismay over trials and deprivations in the Great Depression. College meant life in an extended family; wartime service was another exercise in collective action; afterward, his first serious career was as a public relations writer for General Electric, explaining and promoting the idea that scientific abstractions and technological advances were in everyone's interest—and in being able to justify this interest in layperson's terms, in words everyone could understand. Behind this all stood the model of his family in Indianapolis: pioneering, large and well established, involved in the community's arts and culture as well as its business, and providing the extensive support that only a seemingly limitless group of close and affectionate relatives can. Combined with Vonnegut's studies in anthropology at the University of Chicago immediately after the war, this upbringing had shaped an individual who knew how much of his life depended upon finding and exercising his role in the community, within a functioning social group.

During this initial period of obscurity as a writer, dating from his first published story in 1950 through his lead-up to fame in 1965–67 with the University of Iowa lectureship and the beginning of his essay writing and public speaking, Vonnegut was still a public spokesman, albeit under more limited circumstances. His family life during these years has been outlined in loving detail by his first wife, Jane Vonnegut Yarmolinsky, in *Angels without Wings*. Her specific focus is the way she and Kurt exercised their sense of social responsibility within the form of an extended family: when Kurt's sister and brother-in-law died within days of each other, he and Jane at once adopted their children, turning a family of five into a family of eight overnight. But during these same years Vonnegut was balancing his extremely private profession as a writer (including days alone with his typewriter, when the only person he would see was the mailman bringing either acceptances or, more often, rejections) with public actions: involving himself and his wife in amateur theatrical groups, teaching in a school for emotionally disturbed children (those who had fallen beyond the reach of conventional strategies of education and socialization), and for a short time picking up needed cash by doing some public relations work (specifically translating the masterly achievements of an iron-casting firm into terms the general public could appreciate). That so many of his short stories were drawn from everyday middle-class concerns is unremarkable, given his relatively unwriterly interest in so many mundane activities.

Vonnegut's fiction of the 1950s, as will be seen, remains of a piece with his novel writing of later years thanks to a common dedication to the way the author sees himself and so positions himself in his work: as an individual with a very personal history addressing the public multitudes, conveying to them needed information but in a way that makes it acceptable as friendly, almost intimate advice. That his speaking style itself remained unchanged by fame is evident from a typical appearance during his decade of greatest celebrity, the 1970s. The occasion here is a visit on March 31, 1977, to the University of Northern Iowa—where a former Iowa City student had hosted his appearance eleven years before and where she and several other friends and former students now taught. In those eleven years Kurt Vonnegut had gone from an unknown writer of bus station paperbacks and stories for family magazines to one of the country's best-selling and most eminent authors. Whatever he wrote now received national acclaim, Broadway had hosted his play, and Hollywood produced a major film of the book that had made him famous, *Slaughterhouse-Five*. At the decade's turn he had been treated, much against his will, as a guru to disaffected youth of the student revolution; now, in 1977, he had more willingly assumed the role of public spokesman on a host of much larger issues, issues he felt were of ultimately global importance.

Yet despite the gravity of these issues, which included the political and ecological disasters the author felt were consuming these times, it is the same Kurt Vonnegut who speaks in 1977 as in 1967. At Ohio State University, he had played his own supposedly vulgar status against the solemnly academic nature of the occasion and the audience's intellectual expectations. At Northern Iowa, he starts with the same approach, only transposed to accommodate his change from obscurity to fame. He picks, for example, a title that exploits his listeners' expectations, "Kurt Vonnegut: A Self-Interview." Here, they might suppose, is the zany author of *Cat's Cradle* and *The Sirens of Titan*, ready to reinforce his position as the font of mystic wisdom and offer them subversions of convention and authority. But once again the author uses his technique of catalyzing this relationship with his audience to generate the participatory attention a good speech must have to succeed. As at Ohio State, a good way to do it is by confounding their expectations.

"How many of you," he asks his listeners, "believe in the superiority of meditation, of the inward contemplation recommended by the great Eastern religions?" Around the auditorium hands shoot up as hundreds of eager students among the audience of nearly two thousand seek to identify themselves with him.

"Well, you're all full of crap," Vonnegut tells them, at once deflating their pretensions and correcting one of the more superficial, even inane aspects of his fame. The hand-raisers are shocked, while those who kept their hands in their laps are now both laughing and applauding this only slightly cruel joke played on the less serious among them. The speaker takes part in the laughter, but in a warmly forgiving rather than judgmental way, as if to remind himself that for many years in the late 1960s and early 1970s the joke had been on him. Then comes his justification for this little bit of harmless criticism: that meditation is too passive to produce much good, and that the simpler practice of reading books—and reacting to them imaginatively—is a much better way to grow and learn, even about oneself.

Kurt Vonnegut, of course, is famous for his books—specifically for writing *Slaughterhouse-Five* and seeing it made into a major motion picture. But just as with his misconstrued notoriety as a partisan of meditation and other countercultural practices, he pauses to lament how bestsellerdom and film success contradict his beliefs in how societies best operate. The ideal, he recalls from his studies in anthropology, is to organize in a folk society of about two thousand people. Coincidentally, that is the size of his audience tonight, but it offers a good example of the point he wants to make. Here they are, all two thousand of them, listening to one author—a reminder of the vast national and international audience he serves. Far better than this global community would be smaller yet coherent groups in which there would be a role and meaningful work for everyone, including artists, musicians, and even a few storytellers. But now, in the mass-market culture America must produce, a single musician performs on records and on television for 200 million people. For writers it becomes a case of being a best-seller or going bust. There are just a few who can publish in such circumstances, he says, adding "Thank God I'm one of them!"

For movies it is even worse. A writer hoping for best-seller status can at least get writing on his own; all he or she needs is a pencil and paper, and ultimately the use of a typewriter to get it looking professional enough for a publisher to consider. But for film, the prerequisites are overwhelming. Here the whole process, even once under way, remains so expensive that it is almost impossible to make room for individual expression. In turn, the product is viewed passively by audiences being shown what to imagine. Almost completely lost is the generative power that creates great literature and rewards imaginatively active reading.

At this point the author takes up the printed portion of his text, the "Self-Interview" soon to be published in the *Paris Review* and eventually collected in *Palm Sunday*. The text itself is a patchwork of others, with bits and pieces drawn from four separate interviews done over the years by several different people, none of whom had captured the essence of Kurt Vonnegut's art. From these scraps the speaker assembles a coherent narrative that, as if made to order for this occasion with his audience, explores the nature of interrogating himself. Listener reaction to this process is essential, as the National Public Radio tape of it reveals: Vonnegut using two voices, a normal one for the interviewer and an absurdly choked one for his "own," a comic situation that at once has the audience howling. As he did in Ohio, Vonnegut works his audience by working himself, in each case taking a point of difficulty in public delivery of his material and then making that struggle both a joke and his speech's point. Once more he makes art from his response to life, then tests it and perfects it by trying it out in public, the "audience of strangers" he had always told his writing students to face.

The next decade would be less kind to Kurt Vonnegut. Somewhat like F. Scott Fitzgerald in the 1930s, the conservative 1980s were less fond of Vonnegut's sometimes revolutionary attitudes from an era which had seemed to run its course. Audiences were still at capacity, applauding whichever work-in-progress he would conclude with—*Slaughterhouse-Five* in 1967, *Jailbird* in 1977, or *Bluebeard* later in the 1980s—and such recurrent devices as his story-line chalk talk continued to prompt delight and understanding. The books themselves would be best-sellers, but critics were more hostile than ever. Not surprisingly, the author chose this time to write a requiem mass. Yet even here his intentions were meliorative, transposing the hellfire and damnation of typical sixteenth-century works into happier attitudes of peace and repose. To seal his accomplishment in formal terms he had his *Requiem* translated into Church Latin and set to choral music, the premier performance of which became the occasion for what would be his representative speech of these times.

The speech's title is one used for most of his appearances here and afterward: "How to Get a Job Like Mine." Producer Robert Weide, assembling raw film for a planned documentary on the author, captured it on March 12, 1988, when in preparation for the *Requiem*'s premier by the Buffalo Symphony and choir of that city's Unitarian Universalist Church. For this occasion Vonnegut delivered his talk the night before as a fund-raiser for the musical event. Presented from the cathedral's altar where the *Requiem* would be performed the following evening, it is much the same lecture he would give a year later during his third appearance (in three different decades) at the University of Northern Iowa.

Twelve years older and presumably even wiser, Kurt Vonnegut now comes on as more the grandfatherly type than a father, bringing gentle rather than caustic knowledge to his listeners in hope of making them more comfortable. It was March in Buffalo and early April in Cedar Falls, times of the year when better weather is promised but not yet at hand, and it is this vexation to which the speaker addresses himself. Why does the weather always make us unhappy? Why does it always seem to irritate us so, prompting worry and complaint? The reason is because we have been given the wrong information about it. Just consider how fundamentally off we are. To prove his point, Vonnegut asks a simple question: how many seasons are there? "Four" is the wrong answer. There are actually six—the four that everyone thinks they know about plus two in between: the "Unlocking" of March and April when springtime pleasures are expected but not yet here; and the "Locking" of November and December when Nature starts shutting down to get ready for the deepfreeze of true winter. It is something the speaker learned himself forty years earlier from a friend when living in Schenectady, when March and April did not seem very springlike and November and December had not kept the promise of fall. "I think that you'll be a lot more comfortable on this planet," he assures his listeners, "now that I've told you that."

Wisely comforting advice—with this indication of what his speaker's tone will be, Vonnegut makes further fun of expectations by mocking what a good speech should be. Rules for public speaking, he reminds his listeners, emphasize that the speaker should never apologize. To show how ridiculous such a rule is, he proceeds to apologize—at length and for nothing in particular. "I'm terribly sorry, and feel just awful about it," he says, then runs through a litany of apologies that emphasize how he is quite mortified, it will never happen again, and so forth. By the time he is done, however, he has made the audience love him. As with his little lesson about the weather, a common rule has been broken, only to show how things work better when it is.

In each case Vonnegut has made his point by interacting with his audience. And that interaction conforms to what he has always described as the classic structure for jokes: asking a question, getting a response, then correcting that response with something surprising and therefore funny. It is the way he writes fiction, page after page of setting a bit of energy and then releasing it, all the while incorporating the reader's response as part of the narrative's larger movement. Thus reader and listener alike are asked to take a step, then gently pushed off balance and set in a different direction, with the sum of those redirections being the point Vonnegut wants to make.

His lecture uses many texts, most of which he invites the audience to rewrite. There is no argument about changing the traditional requiem mass into something more soothing and appealing, but from here Vonnegut moves on to the Bible, telling listeners how his own great-grandfather did it with a pamphlet titled *An Instruction in Morals from the Standpoint of a Free*

Thinker, something any open-minded person would find to be a very useful document. In similar manner Vonnegut coaches young writers how to reshape their own attempts at short stories and novels. Even the plot line of American history is blue-pencilled, allowing that the original thirteen colonies and its Continental Congress can hardly be called the birthplace of liberty when slavery was to prevail for almost another century and women would await the granting of equal rights for another two. No, the birth of liberty is happening just now. At best, colonial Philadelphia was where liberty was conceived, not born; better to call it "the motel of liberty."

This gets a laugh, but Vonnegut's point is made. To remind his listeners that he is not imposing jokes where they do not belong, he tells a good one, historically accurate, on Thomas Jefferson. As a libertarian, the author of the Declaration of Independence wished to free his slaves but could not—they were mortgaged. Can his audience imagine Vonnegut, momentarily short of cash, putting his cleaning woman in hock? That is what certain realities of American history ask us to do.

"How to Get a Job Like Mine" ends, as usual, with the author's story-line chalk talk. But in the intervening years since he first presented it the lesson has changed, recognizing what Vonnegut has learned from writing his own canon of works and addressing himself to great public issues. Its first half reveals, as before, the rise-and-fall structure common to fabricated narratives and the delight readers take in it. This time through, however, he contrasts such extreme patterns to the essentially flat nature of primitive tales, in which there are no perceptible highs and lows but simply level progress. As opposed to what appears to be the flat-line boredom of Native American narratives, Vonnegut traces with great exuberance the roller-coaster fortunes of Cinderella. The latter, obviously, is the more entertaining—which leads him to ask his listeners a question: to which pattern does great literature conform? To find out, he puts Shakespeare's *Hamlet* to such a test, and shows—to the audience's great amazement—that its trajectory is just as flat as any primitive tale. There are no great rises or falls to Hamlet's fortune, no way of telling whether one incident or another is "good news" or "bad news."

Does this mean, as Vonnegut asks, "that Shakespeare couldn't write any better than an Indian?" That is the wrong question to ask, he cautions, because the genius both of the English language's greatest writer and of the culturally central tales preserved by primitive societies is that each recognizes the truth about life. That truth is clear and simple: how life appears flat to us because we do not know what is the good news and what is the bad. Yet to make sense of life we tell ourselves that we do, and we impose all sorts of defining structures that yield pleasurable (but ultimately false) tales such as

"Cinderella" and countless other civilized narratives in the form of fiction, movies, and television shows.

Who would think that these popular entertainments are dangerous? But they are, because they lead us to become bored with our lives when these lives are found lacking in the delightful variations of "good stories"; and once so bored, we feel driven to great mischief to liven things up. It is a weakness that reaches from family life to national politics, including the doings of the current administration that gets the country into a little trouble (Grenada), gets it out again, and then repeats the process (in Panama) as a manageable amusement ride, when in fact the proper role of government is to keep things securely stable.

Thus Kurt Vonnegut's public spokesmanship takes the same course as his fiction: indicating the assumptions that lie behind our most firmly held convictions. As such, he qualifies as a deconstructionist, sharing the habit of thought common to our age. The roots for this disposition can be traced back to the firebombing of Dresden, where many scientific and cultural principles of his education were dismantled in an orgy of physical destruction and moral contradiction. Such were the matters Vonnegut spoke about on May 3, 1990, at the Smithsonian Institution's Air and Space Museum for its program of lectures and films on "The Legacy of Strategic Bombing." Here he appeared not only as the author of *Slaughterhouse-Five* but as a victim of aerial bombardment, just the opposite role of the next month's speaker, bombing strategist Gen. Curtis E. LeMay. The novel had been conceived as an act of witness to the Dresden event, and the difficulty of articulating such unspeakableness had determined its structure and generated its ideas—just as the professed difficulties of speaking at Columbus, Cedar Falls, and Buffalo had set the formats and bridged understandings with his audiences there. At the Smithsonian the same thing would happen.

For this new decade of activity Vonnegut would move to integrate his roles of writing and public spokesmanship. Increasing mention would be made of such issues as politics and the environment even as they assumed thematic importance in the novel being worked on at the time, *Hocus Pocus*. Dresden is given repeated emphasis as something not just central to his fictive canon but pertinent to such concerns as the invasion of Panama and the ecological catastrophe of global warming. Yet even as Kurt Vonnegut approaches the podium with these and other matters in mind, the specific occasion of delivering this speech intrudes and determines his strategy for all that follows.

The circumstance is one of surprise, being informed that in attendance tonight, sitting in the second row, is his colleague from prisoner-of-war days in Dresden's slaughterhouse number 5, Tom Jones. This remarkable coincidence, reaching back to events forty-five years past and yet on the docket for tonight's appearance, lets Vonnegut transform his lecture into something well beyond its printed text. He is able to do so by relying on what has come to be his customary manner, improvising a public talk the same way his personal fictions are constructed and then tested out. In each case his method has been to involve the audience, posing questions and challenging assumptions. With a bonafide participant from Dresden in this audience, the speaker is able both to strengthen existing points and improvise new ones, discovering fresh truths in the process and sharing them with listeners who are themselves witnesses to Vonnegut and Jones's reunion. This process is similar to the way he was cross-referencing historical materials in *Hocus Pocus*, and it anticipates how he would use Tom Jones's material in *Fates Worse than Death* the next year.

"You're still alive!" Kurt Vonnegut exclaims as he reads the note and spots Tom Jones down in front. "How nice!" As a spontaneous and inevitably offhand remark, this confirms the speaker's thesis even before he had a chance to state it: that there is nothing intelligent to say about a massacre. In *Slaughterhouse-Five* the response is to listen to the birds chirping; here, it is what any old-timer might say to another he has bumped into after many years. More than 150,000 human beings were wiped out at Dresden; Tom and Kurt were not; and as for finding a reason for this, there is nothing much more to be said than "So it goes." As Vonnegut will explain, strategic bombing works much like germ eradication, with any chance for individual consideration about surviving the disinfectant being lost in the greater general purpose—a purpose that even in military terms often lacks meaning beyond the reflexes of anger and revenge. It was a pure accident that Kurt Vonnegut survived, just as it is an accident now that both he and Tom Jones have lived so many years afterward and meet here tonight. Such meeting can only produce a similar reflex—"How nice!" But like the "*Poo-tee-wheet?*" of birdsong after the Dresden firestorm, it is the most sensible appraisal of strategic bombing that can be made.

What does survive is the human bond, and with Tom Jones present Kurt Vonnegut has a perfect example of what he means. Throughout the speech that follows Jones will be called upon for a witness's confirmation. He begins with his familiar joke with the first rule of public speaking, that one must never apologize, and adds that this is probably the first rule for strategic bombing as well. Then he explains that because he has been a critic of Allied bombing, it is always necessary to prove how he was as opposed to Nazi aggression as any patriotic American. In the past Vonnegut would mention how he served in the army and was taken prisoner at the Battle of the Bulge. Now he can look up from his text and say he is glad that Tom is here to tell what a brave soldier he was, "how hard I fought before being subdued," something that encourages his listeners to break into laughter at this obvious ploy of old buddies exaggerating their war stories. Later, after detailing the Dresden raid and what he saw there, Vonnegut departs once again from his script to say "So was Tom. See, this is all true! I could be snowing you. This is the truth, isn't it, Tom?" From this point on Tom Jones becomes part of the speech, every "I" becoming a "we," every "me" now an "us."

Such extension helps make Vonnegut's point about how the Dresden raid's victimization is related to subsequent bombing in Cambodia, in Vietnam, and most recently in Panama, in reference to which the speaker mentions a casualty figure of four thousand. He asks how many others in this audience have been bombed from the air and sees several hands go up, proving his point that "it is not a very exclusive club." Yet it is a club of individual people and not just statistics. Vonnegut describes the attack on Libya's Muammar Qaddafi that wound up killing his adopted daughter, "the same age and degree of innocence as my own adopted daughter"—who, like Tom Jones, is present tonight and can be pointed out. Here is where individuality lies: not in strategic bombing's symbol of national pride, "like the Liberty Bell," but rather as a practice that kills real people, most of them haplessly innocent.

But simply to protest against war does no more good than protesting against a glacier, as Vonnegut himself was reminded when writing the first chapter of *Slaughterhouse-Five*. His listeners need something practical, and so just as at Ohio State when he checklisted the best books they could read, he now evaluates which cities should and should not have been bombed. "No" for Dresden, as has been credibly established. "Yes," to his audience's surprise, for the other German city destroyed in a firestorm, Hamburg—a defensible answer because the target did have military importance. By the same manner of thinking Hiroshima is checked off "Yes" while Nagasaki rates a "No." After that, through America's subsequent wars, every other city is judged "No" because they were inappropriate targets, from Hanoi and places in Cambodia to more recent attacks on Libya ("That was show biz") and Panama ("That was more show biz").

In both his fiction and his public speaking Kurt Vonnegut begins as very much the personalist. But never is mere confession or simple autobiography his method; rather, his way is to engage this personal self in larger issues. In *Slaughterhouse-Five* that issue is not just the book's subject but his own struggle in finding a way to write about it, just as in all his speeches he makes use of his present circumstances (at Ohio State, obscurity; at the University of Northern Iowa, misconstrued celebrity; at Buffalo, grandfatherly wisdom; at the Smithsonian, encountering Tom Jones) to involve his audience with what is made of this occasion. By the 1990s, with Vonnegut in his sixth decade as a writer and fourth as a public speaker, he comes full circle to the matter of Dresden, not just identifying Joe Crone as the model for Billy Pilgrim but visiting the grave in Rochester, New York, to which Joe's parents had brought his remains. Talking about this at the University of New Orleans on the fiftieth anniversary of V-E Day, the author shared his experience with novelist Joseph Heller and historian Stephen Ambrose, telling these fellow veterans what it meant: "I was deeply moved, and it finally closed out the Second World War for me completely."

Vonnegut's novels are much like his speeches, built on the implications of an audience attending to the author's foibles and weaknesses as well as taking cues from his strengths. With a real, live audience present, one can witness Vonnegut proposing and responding, acting and reacting, drawing on his own experience to meld it with the experiences of his listeners in order to create a work that succeeds as performance. In each speech one hears the vernacular American voice that first became a literary mode with Mark Twain, but which performed national service as well for Abraham Lincoln and Will Rogers as those great public spokesmen counseled the country through its two greatest crises, the Civil War and the Great Depression. Like the finest of American art in all genres, his speeches are improvised and even a bit cobbled together—yet based on an individuality of character and delight in personality that audiences are forever willing to share.

Reminded of Granville Hicks's comments twenty-one years after they were made, Kurt Vonnegut remarked that "It really makes a difference, I find, if people hear me speak." His governing tactics and strategies as a writer have been to make his readers hear, an ideal approach for conveying in his personal fictions what turn out to be urgently public messages.

Chronology

1922   Kurt Vonnegut Jr. born November 11 in Indianapolis, Indiana, son of architect Kurt Vonnegut and Edith Leiber Vonnegut. He has an older brother, Bernard, and a sister, Alice.

1929   Vonnegut family fortune disappears as the Great Depression begins.

1936   Enters Shortridge High School, where he becomes editor of the school's daily newspaper, the *Echo*, before graduating in 1940.

1940   Enrolls at Cornell University, majoring in chemistry and biology; becomes columnist and managing editor of the college's newspaper, the *Cornell Daily Sun*.

1943   Enlists in the United States Army.

1944   Mother commits suicide on May 14, Mother's Day; assigned to U.S. Army's 106th Infantry Division; on December 19, becomes German prisoner of war after being captured at Battle of the Bulge, and is sent to Dresden, an "open city" presumably not threatened with Allied attack.

1945   Survives the Allied firebombing of Dresden, February 13–14, in which over 130,000 are killed; freed from imprisonment May

22; marries Jane Marie Cox on September 1; moves to Chicago in December.

1946   Works as a reporter for the Chicago City News Bureau and undertakes graduate studies in anthropology at the university of Chicago.

1947   Leaves graduate school without a degree; takes a job as a publicist for General Electric.

1950   First short story, "Report on the Barnhouse Effect," is published in *Collier's* magazine.

1951   Quits job; moves to Massachusetts to write full-time.

1952   First novel, *Player Piano*, is published by Scribner's; sells short stories to magazines, including *Collier's* and the *Saturday Evening Post*.

1954–56 Teaches English at the Hopefield School on Cape Cod.

1957   Father dies on October 1.

1958   Sister Alice dies of cancer and her husband dies in a train accident; the Vonneguts adopt three children.

1959   *The Sirens of Titan* is published.

1961   *Canary in a Cat House*, a collection of short stories, is published.

1962   *Mother Night* is published.

1963   *Cat's Cradle* is published.

1965   *God Bless You, Mr. Rosewater* is published; begins a two-year residency at the University of Iowa Writers' Workshop.

1967   Awarded a Guggenheim Fellowship; undertakes a return visit to Dresden.

1968   A collection of short stories, *Welcome to the Monkey House*, is published.

1969   *Slaughterhouse-Five, or The Children's Crusade*, Vonnegut's account of the firebombing of Dresden, is published and quickly becomes a bestseller.

1970   Teaches creative writing at Harvard University. Writes *Happy Birthday, Wanda June*, a play.

1971   Receives a Master's degree in anthropology from the University of Chicago; moves to New York.

1972   "Between Time and Timbuktu" produced as a television special by National Educational Television; son Mark suffers a schizophrenic breakdown, which forms the basis for Mark's 1975 book, *The Eden Express: A Personal Account of Schizophrenia*; film version of *Slaughterhouse-Five* produced.

1973   *Breakfast of Champions, or Goodbye, Blue Monday!* is published; appointed Distinguished Professor on English Prose at the City University of New York.

1974   *Wampeters, Foma, and Granfalloons: Opinions*, a collection of essays, speeches, and reviews, is published.

1976   *Slapstick, or Lonesome No More!* is published; the book is a critical failure.

1979   *Jailbird* published; first marriage ends in divorce; marries photographer Jill Krementz.

1980   A children's book, *Sun Moon Star*, is published in collaboration with illustrator Ivan Chermayeff.

1981   *Palm Sunday: An Autobiographical Collage* is published.

1982   *Deadeye Dick* published; *Fates Worse Than Death* published in England as pamphlet, by Bertrand Russell Peace Foundation.

1985   *Galapágos* published.

1986   Former wife Jane Vonnegut Yarmolinsky dies of cancer in December.

1987   *Bluebeard* published; *Angels without Wings: A Courageous Family's Triumph over Tragedy,* by Jane Vonnegut Yarmolinsky, published. It is the story of adopting and raising her sister-in-law's children.

1988   *Requiem,* a musical piece, is performed by the Buffalo Symphony.

1990   *Hocus Pocus* is published.

1991   *Even Worse Than Death: An Autobiographical Collage of the 1980's* is published; with wife Jill Krementz, files petition for divorce; it is later withdrawn.

1996   Robert Weide's film adaptation of *Mother Night* is released nationally by Fine Line Features; a stage adaptation of *Slaughterhouse-Five* premiers at the Steppenwolf Theatre Company in Chicago.

1997   *Timequake,* which Vonnegut claims will be his last novel, is published; brother Bernard dies.

1999   Film version of *Breakfast of Champions* is distributed in limited release.

Contributors

HAROLD BLOOM is Sterling Professor of the Humanities at Yale University and Henry W. and Albert A. Berg Professor of English at the New York University Graduate School. He is the author of over 20 books, including *Shelley's Mythmaking* (1959), *The Visionary Company* (1961), *Blake's Apocalypse* (1963), *Yeats* (1970), *A Map of Misreading* (1975), *Kabbalah and Criticism* (1975), *Agon: Toward a Theory of Revisionism* (1982), *The American Religion* (1992), *The Western Canon* (1994), and *Omens of Millennium: The Gnosis of Angels, Dreams, and Resurrection* (1996). *The Anxiety of Influence* (1973) sets forth Professor Bloom's provocative theory of the literary relationships between the great writers and their predecessors. His most recent books include *Shakespeare: The Invention of the Human*, a 1998 National Book Award finalist, and *How to Read and Why*, which was published in 2000. In 1999, Professor Bloom received the prestigious American Academy of Arts and Letters Gold Medal for Criticism.

PETER J. REED published the first book-length study of Kurt Vonnegut Jr. in 1972. Originally from England (where he served in the Royal Air Force), he now lives in Minneapolis, where he teaches English at the University of Minnesota.

PETER G. JONES is a Lieutenant Colonel in the U.S. Army. He has taught in the English department at the United States Military Academy at West Point, and currently works in the U.S. Army's Enlisted Evacuation Center at Fort Benjamin Harrison, Indiana.

JAMES LUNDQUIST is a professor of English at St. Cloud State University in Minnesota. He is the author of books on Sinclair Lewis, Theodore Dreiser, and Chester Himes.

ROBERT MERRILL has written articles for such scholarly publications as *American Literature* and *Indiana English Journal*. He teaches at the University of Nevada, Reno.

PETER A. SCHOLL is a professor of English at the University of Evansville, Michigan. His essays have been published in *American Literature* and *Indiana English Journal*.

LAWRENCE R. BROER is a professor of English at the University of South Florida. He is the author of *Hemingway's Spanish Tragedy* and *Sanity Plea: Schizophrenia in the Novels of Kurt Vonnegut*, as well as contributor to numerous anthologies of literary criticism.

LEONARD MUSTAZZA is a professor of English at the Ogontz Campus of the Pennsylvania State University. His books include *Such Prompt Eloquence: Language as Agency and Character in Milton's Epics*.

WILLIAM RODNEY ALLEN teaches English at the Louisiana School for Math, Science, and the Arts. He is the author of *Walker Percy: A Southern Wayfarer* and editor of *Conversations with Kurt Vonnegut*.

JEROME KLINKOWITZ is the author of more than thirty books, including novels, collections of short stories, and studies in philosophy, art, music, sports, and literature. His literary studies include several books and articles on Kurt Vonnegut Jr. He is a professor of English and University Distinguished Scholar at the University of Northern Iowa.

Bibliography

Aldridge, Alexandra. *The Scientific World View in Dystopia.* Ann Arbor, Mich.: UMI Research Press, 1984.

Allen, William Rodney. *Understanding Kurt Vonnegut.* Columbia: University of South Carolina Press, 1991.

Berryman, Charles. "After the Fall: Kurt Vonnegut." *Critique* 26 (1985): 96–102.

Bianculli, David. "The Theory of Evolution According to Vonnegut." *The Philadelphia Inquirer* (10 November 1985): S6.

Broer, Lawrence R. *Sanity Plea: Schizophrenia in the Novels of Kurt Vonnegut.* Ann Arbor, Mich.: UMI Research Press, 1989.

Bryan, C. D. B. "Kurt Vonnegut, Head Bokononist," *New York Times Book Review* (6 April 1969): 2, 25.

Buck, Lynn. "Vonnegut's World of Comic Futility." *Studies in American Fiction* 3 (1975): 181–98.

Chabot, C. Barry. "Slaughterhouse-Five and the Comforts of Indifference." *Essays in Literature* 8 (1981): 45–51.

Eliade, Mircea. *Myth and Reality.* Translated by Willard R. Trask. New York: Harper and Row, 1963.

Fiedler, Leslie A. "The Divine Stupidity of Kurt Vonnegut." *Esquire* (September 1970): 195–197; 199–200; 202–4.

Giannone, Richard. *Vonnegut: A Preface to His Novels.* Port Washington, N.Y.: Kennikat, 1977.

Goldsmith, David H. *Kurt Vonnegut: Fantasist of Fire and Ice.* Bowling Green, Ohio: Bowling Green University Popular Press, 1972.

Harris, Charles B. *Contemporary Novelists of the Absurd.* New Haven, Conn.: College and University Press, 1971.

Hipkiss, Robert A. *The American Absurd: Pynchon, Vonnegut, and Barth.* Port Washington, N.Y.: Associated Faculty Press, 1984.

Hume, Kathryn. *Fantasy and Mimesis: Responses to Reality in Western Literature.* London: Methuen, 1984.

Ihab, Hassan. *Contemporary American Literature 1945–1972.* New York: Frederick Ungar, 1973.

133

Karl, Frederick. *American Fictions: 1940–1980*. New York: Harper and Row, 1983.
Klinkowitz, Jerome. *Kurt Vonnegut*. London: Methuen, 1982.
————. *Literary Disruptions: The Making of a Post-Contemporary American Fiction*. Urbana: University of Illinois Press, 1975.
Lewis, R. W. B. *The American Adam: Innocence Tragedy and Tradition in American Literature*. Chicago: University of Chicago Press, 1955.
Lundquist, James. *Kurt Vonnegut*. New York: Frederick Ungar, 1977.
May, John R. "Vonnegut's Humor and the Limits of Hope." *Twentieth Century Literature* 18 (1972): 25–36.
Mayo, Clark. *Kurt Vonnegut: The Gospel from Outer Space*. San Bernadino, Calif.: Borgo Press, 1977.
McGinnis, Wayne D. "The Arbitrary Cycle of *Slaughterhouse-Five*." *Critique* 17 (1975): 55–68.
Merril, Robert, and Peter A. Scholl. "Vonnegut's *Slaughterhouse-Five*: The Requirements of Chaos." *Studies in American Fiction* 6 (1978): 65–76.
Myers, David. "Kurt Vonnegut, Jr.: Morality-Myth in the Antinovel." *International Fiction Review* 3 (1976): 52–56.
Nigro, August J. *The Diagonal Line: Separation and Reparation in American Literature*. Selinsgrove, Pa.: Susquehanna University Press, 1984.
Reed, Peter J. *Kurt Vonnegut, Jr.* New York: Warner, 1972.
Samuels, Charles. "Age of Vonnegut." *The New Republic* (12 June 1971): 30–32.
Schatt, Stanley. *Kurt Vonnegut, Jr.* Boston: Twayne, 1976.
Schriber, Mary Sue. "Bringing Chaos to Order: The Novel Tradition and Kurt Vonnegut Jr." *Genre* 10 (1977): 283–97.
Spivey, Ted R. *The Journey Beyond Tragedy: A Study of Myth and Modern Fiction*. Orlando: University Presses of Florida, 1980.
Tanner, Tony. *City of Words: American Fiction 1950–1970*. New York: Harper and Row, 1971.
White, John J. *Mythology in the Modern Novel: A Study of Prefigurative Technique*. Princeton, N.J.: Princeton University Press, 1971.
Wolfe, G. K. "Vonnegut and the Metaphor of Science Fiction." *Journal of Popular Culture* 5 (1972): 964–69.

Acknowledgments

"The End of the Road: *Slaughterhouse-Five, or The Children's Crusade*" by Peter J. Reed. From *Kurt Vonnegut, Jr.* © 1972 by Warner Books, Inc. Reprinted with permission.

"At War with Technology: Kurt Vonnegut, Jr." by Peter G. Jones. From *War and the Novelist: Appraising the American War Novel.* © 1976 by the Curators of the University of Missouri. Reprinted with permission.

"The 'New Reality' of *Slaughterhouse-Five*" by James Lundquist. From *Kurt Vonnegut.* © 1977 by Frederick Ungar Publishing Co., Inc. Reprinted with permission of the Continuum Publishing Company.

"Vonnegut's *Slaughterhouse-Five*: The Requirements of Chaos" by Robert Merrill and Peter A. Scholl. From *Studies in American Fiction* 6, no. 1 (Spring 1978). © 1978 by Northeastern University. Reprinted with permission.

"*Slaughterhouse-Five*: Pilgrim's Progress" by Lawrence R. Broer. From *Sanity Plea: Schizophrenia in the Novels of Kurt Vonnegut.* © 1989 by Lawrence R. Broer. Reprinted with permission.

"Adam and Eve in the Golden Depths: Edenic Madness in *Slaughterhouse-Five*" by Leonard Mustazza. From *Forever Pursuing Genesis: The Myth of Eden in the Novels of Kurt Vonnegut.* © 1990 by Associated University Presses, Inc. Reprinted with permission.

"Slaughterhouse-Five" by William Rodney Allen. From *Understanding Kurt Vonnegut.* © 1991 University of South Carolina. Reprinted with permission.

"Emerging from Anonymity" by Jerome Klinkowitz. From *Vonnegut in Fact: The Public Spokesmanship of Personal Fiction.* © 1998 University of South Carolina. Reprinted with permission.

Index

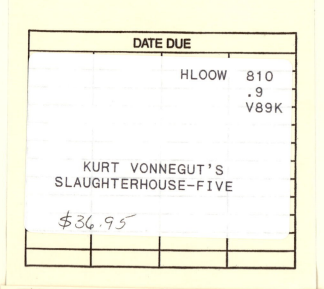